ETHIOPIA

The Country That Cut Off Its Head

A Diary of the Revolution

BLAIR THOMSON

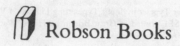 Robson Books

FIRST PUBLISHED IN GREAT BRITAIN IN 1975 BY ROBSON
BOOKS LTD., 28 POLAND STREET, LONDON W1V 3DB.
COPYRIGHT © 1975 BLAIR THOMSON.

ISBN 0 903895 50 1

Computer Typeset by Input Typesetting Limited, 4 Valentine Place,
London SE1 Printed in Great Britain by Hazell Watson and Viney
Limited, Aylesbury

To my wife
FAITH
for living through the
revolution, living through
this book, and living up to her name

And with thanks to
ALASTAIR MORRELL (BBC)
DOUGLAS SCOTT   (*Daily Express*)
GAVIN ANDREW   (*The Observer*)
PHILIP CAMPBELL   (ABC Radio Network)
HENRY VALTOS   (*The Times*)
A. NON   (*Time Magazine*)

ACKNOWLEDGEMENTS

The author wishes to thank Bill Lee for his friendship, inspiration and invaluable assistance, Barry Maughan for being such a good colleague to work with in Ethiopia, and Larry Hodgson, Donald Milner, George Bennett and Graham Tayar of the BBC for their help and encouragement.

And a very special thanks to the people of Ethiopia — especially those whose friendship I value most, but whose names I dare not print.

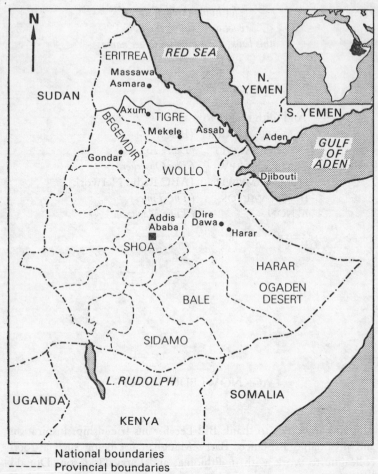

—·—	National boundaries
----	Provincial boundaries
——	Eritrean boundary

CONTENTS

AUTHOR'S NOTE

This book makes no attempt to be a definitive study of Ethiopia or a comprehensive analysis of its revolution. Indeed, I have had to force myself to leave out much that was interesting but not necessarily crucial to the development of the revolution, and instead, concentrate on the main events. Drawing on personal experience, I have tried to retell it as it happened. I have also tried to transmit to the reader some of the drama, excitement and fascination of what will undoubtedly be recorded as one of the most momentous periods in the history of Ethiopia.

At one level, Ethiopia's protracted revolution stands on its own as a story of mystery, intrigue, duplicity and murder, set in a wild and fascinating country. But it is also the latest chapter in a long history of turbulence in a land that is still largely unknown. The revolution can only be properly understood in the light of that history, and of the nature and cultures of the many ethnic groupings whose once independent kingdoms were loosely brought together into the Ethiopian Empire. A short section on the history of Ethiopia, the country and its people is therefore included to set the scene for the events that were to produce the 'Creeping Coup'.

Names have sometimes been omitted to protect people still in Ethiopia and still at risk from the authorities.

At the very least, it is hoped that this book will give the reader a better understanding of the events and country behind the headlines.

April 1975   BLAIR THOMSON

1 Historical Background

'Ethiopia is a mystery in the hands of God'
– Haile Selassie, July 1972

One of the frequent claims made by the Ethiopian military authorities both during and immediately after the 'Creeping Coup' stage of the revolution was that they wanted to turn their backs on the 'three thousand years of history' so often referred to by Emperor Haile Selassie. Yet one of the favourite souvenirs thrust on the visitor to Addis Ababa is a handpainted scroll depicting a meeting between the Queen of Sheba and King Solomon. In pre-revolution days, loyal Ethiopians were inordinately proud of the legend – which they accepted as fact – that Emperor Haile Selassie was the 225th successive monarch of a dynasty established by a love affair between Solomon and Sheba.

Easier to establish is the fact that the earliest people to inhabit the country we know as Ethiopia were the descendants of the family of Ham, the son of Noah – in particular of Ham's son, Cush, who in Ethiopian history is called 'Ethiops'. Not long after the Cushites settled in the northern Ethiopian highlands, they were joined – and eventually dominated – by Semitic tribes from Southern Arabia, one of which, the Habesha, gave the country a new name – Habesh, or Abyssinia.

The joint kingdom formed by the Cushites and the Arabian Semites established its capital at Axum in northern Ethiopia. By the third century AD the kings of Axum had founded the beginnings of the Ethiopian empire by conquering the areas which now comprise the provinces of northern Eritrea, Begemdir, the Danakil region, and southern Tigre.

It was about this time that Christianity first came to Ethiopia – and in a rather bizarre fashion. The story goes that a Syrian merchant, on his way to India, put in for food and water at what is now the Eritrean coastline of the Red Sea. He and all his crew were killed, but two boys escaped. They were Christians, and one of them, Frumentius, so impressed the king of Ethiopia that he became the royal secretary. When the king died, Frumentius was asked to help rule the kingdom until the heir to the throne was old enough to take over, and used his position to found a Christian community.

In the 7th century an over-enthusiastic Ethiopian army invaded the coast of Arabia and threatened to destroy the city of Mecca, spiritual home of the young and thrusting religion of Islam. Thus began more than a thousand years of conflict between Christians and Moslems. The latter spread into Eritrea, and through Somalia into the southern provinces of Ethiopia, occupied by the warlike Oromo people (later to be better known by their Amharic name – Gallas).

One king in particular – Amde Tsion, who ruled in the first half of the fourteenth century – scored many successes against the Moslems. By this time the capital had moved south to Lalibella, and Christianity had taken a firm hold in the central part of Ethiopia, in Gojjam and in what is now Shoa province, at the centre of which stands the present capital, Addis Ababa. The people of these provinces were the Amharas, and even at this early stage they were the most politically instructed people of Ethiopia and deeply committed to the Coptic religion. Amde Tsion recognized their two-fold value – and extended his sphere of influence, gaining strong Christian support against the Moslems by enlisting their help. In the years that followed, the Amharas were to become the dominant force in deciding who would rule Ethiopia, what form of government it would take, and what the official language and religion would be. Their power was not to be broken until the 1974 revolution.

For a hundred years after the rule of Amde Tsion, the kings of Ethiopia consolidated their position, still fighting off Moslem incursions, and still largely cut off from the rest of the world, until news began to filter through to the West of a great and wise king referred to as Prester John. This appears to have been Zera Yakob, a remarkable king who ruled Ethiopia for thirty-four years and who laid the foundations of the country's feudal system, despite his being in his day quite a reformer. He encouraged the writing of books, and established a kind of national system of government, dividing up his empire into provinces, each ruled by a nobleman called a Ras (the equivalent of an English duke) who was also head of the army in his own province. Zera Yakob was also a devout Christian, and the whole educational structure of the country, such as it was, was based on the church.

Portuguese explorers searching for Prester John eventually reached Ethiopia and established links with Europe.

For the next two hundred years kings came and went, all of them fighting the Moslems and the Gallas with varying degrees of success. Ethiopia moved into the second half of the eighteenth century with its kings now housed in Gondar, but with the fiercely independent Rases of areas like Shoa, Gojjam and Tigre largely going their own way, and with the Moslems ruling the Red Sea coast and the eastern province of Harar and the Gallas ruling the south.

By 1850, after the hundred-year-long 'Age of the Rases', no one was quite sure who ruled Ethiopia — and it is likely that no one did. While the Rases jockeyed for position a totally unknown young man began to emerge to threaten them all. His name was Kassa, and after a chequered early life in which his family was left destitute and his monastery home burned by Gallas, he gathered some friends together and set about robbing rich Moslem merchants and building up a powerful private army.

Ras Ali of Gondar tried to stop him, failed, and was forced, for his own survival, to recognize Kassa as governor of the sub-province of Kwara and to give him his daughter in marriage. But Kassa had even greater ambitions, and gradually defeated first the less powerful Ras of Gojjam, and then Ras Ali himself, to become the undisputed ruler of Gojjam and the Amhara lands. The Ras of Tigre thought he'd take advantage of Ras Ali's misfortune to get himself crowned as Emperor, but Kassa intercepted the Patriarch of the Orthodox Church on his way to the ceremony, and forced the terrified churchman to crown him Emperor instead! Kassa went on to defeat the Ras of Tigre and named himself 'negus negiste' – King of Kings – on February 7, 1855.

Now there had long been a prophecy that a great king named Tewodros (Theodore) would bring peace and righteousness to the country. Unwilling to disappoint history, Kassa promptly changed his name to Tewodros, and set about enlarging his empire. He dethroned King Yohannes III, the last King of Gondar, then went to Shoa and unseated King Haile Malakot.

Tewodros moved his capital further south still, to Debre Tabor, and with the aim of making Ethiopia better known in the world, began a period of intense diplomatic activity. He was more active than diplomatic, however, and when Queen Victoria failed to reply to a letter, Tewodros promptly arrested several Englishmen working in Ethiopia. The Queen was not amused, and sent Sir Robert Napier to teach Tewodros a lesson. It took him and the British Army some months to cross the highlands from the Red Sea to Debre Tabor, but they finally attacked the capital. When Tewodros realized the battle was lost, he shot himself. For three years, the Ethiopians were without a ruler. Eventually another Kassa – Ras Kassa of Tigre – emerged triumphant from the power struggle and was crowned as Emperor Yohannes IV in 1872.

Yohannes consolidated his position as emperor by agreeing to let King Haile Malakot's son Menelik keep the title 'King of Shoa' as long as he himself could be 'King of Kings'. He also nominated kings to govern Gondar, Begemdir and Tigre, and following precedent, married his son, Araya Selassie, to King Menelik's daughter Zauditu. It wasn't long, however, before Yohannes – who had early on in his reign fought off Egyptian invaders with British help – was facing more threats from outside. The Italians bought the Red Sea port of Assab – on the coast of what is now Eritrea – from its Sultan, and from this base they tried to invade Ethiopia They also tried to get King Menelik to join them against Emperor Yohannes. They failed in both ploys. Meanwhile, having defeated and killed General Gordon, the Sudanese pushed eastwards, entered Ethiopia and killed Emperor Yohannes in battle in March 1889.

There was again a hiatus as far as the Emperor's throne was concerned. King Menelik of Shoa and Ras Mengesha of Tigre both claimed the throne. Menelik defeated Mengesha but allowed him to stay as governor of Tigre, and Menelik was proclaimed Emperor Menelik II.

His first act was to sign a treaty with the Italians, who thought it meant they controlled Ethiopia, and happily handed over a load of arms to Emperor Menelik's emissary to Rome, Ras Makonnen (father of the man who was to become Emperor Haile Selassie). But they learned their mistake when Menelik began to receive officials from France and Russia. By this time European nations had become more and more interested in lands around Ethiopia, and the British had colonized part of Somalia. The Italians therefore expanded from their base in Assab and took much of Eritrea, deciding once again to attack the highlands of Ethiopia. The attack united the Rases and the Galla peoples behind Menelik and at the battle of Adowa the Italians were routed – an event still celebrated annually in Ethiopia. The result of the battle was a new treaty which, among other things, established the boundary between Ethiopia and Eritrea – creating a running sore that was to contribute to events in Eritrea eighty years later.

Menelik was a reformer and the father of modern Ethiopia. He built a new capital at a place called Finfini, and renamed it Addis Ababa. He instigated the building of a railway between Addis Ababa and the French territorial port of Djibouti on the Gulf of Aden, though he died before the first train puffed its way up the 8,500 feet from sea level to the new capital.

Menelik welcomed help and advice from the West, developed Addis Ababa as a major trading centre, and clarified Ethiopia's boundaries. Just before he died in 1908 he called his Rases together and named his grandson, Iyassu, as heir. Iyassu was only twelve when Menelik died, and Ethiopia was again left with a power vacuum and a struggle among the Rases whose influence Menelik had tried to curb.

In February 1917 Iyassu's reign was abruptly ended and Menelik's daughter Zauditu became Empress, naming young Ras Tafari Makonnen – the man destined to become Haile Selassie – as regent and heir.

2 Haile Selassie – Martyr or Monster?

For most people it will be impossible to think of Ethiopia for many years to come without thinking of Haile Selassie. Not since the Middle Ages has one ruler so stamped his personality for so long on a nation, and indeed, the Middle Ages are really where Emperor Haile Selassie belonged.

The great-grandson of King Sahle Selassie, and son of Ras Makonnen – Menelik's cousin and one of his ablest generals and governors – the young Tafari was a provincial governor by the age of sixteen. In his ten years as regent this well-educated and somewhat impatient young man with his radical, reforming, internationalist views succeeded not only in improving Ethiopia in many ways, but in alienating the traditionally conservative Rases. In October 1928 he assumed the title of 'King', stepped up his reform programme, and provoked the northern Rases into open rebellion in 1930. He defeated them in battle at Debre Tabor, but the event precipitated the death of Empress Zauditu, and on November 2, 1930 Tafari Makonnen was crowned Emperor, taking the name Haile Selassie – which means 'Might of the Princes'.

While Haile Selassie began as a fearless reformer, the sheer weight of tradition in Ethiopia eventually forced him to compromise, as so many of his predecessors had done. He wanted to modernize the country, and sent many young men abroad to gain the education and skills that would help him achieve his aim. Yet he also had to pacify the arch-conservative noblemen and knew that if he tried to do too much too soon, he would probably provoke another open rebellion. He granted a constitution in 1955 – but left some power in the hands of the Rases, and, as Emperor, ensured that he had even more power.

It was almost as if, after his coronation, he developed a kind of schizophrenia. His centralizing of the administration was aimed less at greater efficiency than at giving him tighter control of his fragmented empire, and limiting the opportunities for provincial rulers to rise against him. He established a parliament – but only allowed it to function according to his wishes, and banned political parties.

Throughout the '40s and '50s he presented Ethiopia as an example of a progressive, stable African nation – a rarity in the emerging continent – and few visitors could see beyond the charisma of this diminutive monarch to the harsh realities of his country, with its enormous gap between rich and poor and the blatant corruption.

While presiding over the unification of Ethiopia, he and his system were also largely responsible for ensuring that it was never fully integrated. And in that system were the seeds of his own destruction. He trusted no one and no one trusted him. His detractors didn't trust each other, of course, but it was inevitable that some forces would eventually unite long enough to overthrow him.

Several such attempts were indeed made, the most notable being in 1960. The coup began on December 13, 1960 while the Emperor was on a visit to Brazil, and within a few hours the rebels had control of Addis Ababa, and had arrested several leading members of the regime. They also detained the Crown Prince, Asfa Wossen, and persuaded him to broadcast anti-establishment statements and to declare that he would become a salaried monarch. The 'Red' Ras Imru – a well-known socialist – was pressed into allowing himself to be declared Prime Minister. Within two days, however, a successful counter-coup had been organized and the Emperor returned to find the country back in loyal hands.

The 1960 coup had had little to do with the mass of the population. It had been a struggle between rival factions in the establishment and the military, aimed more at ousting Haile Selassie than ending the feudal regime. However, the attempted coup forced the regime to acknowledge the need for reforms, and although none was ever put into practice, the climate created by the episode gave renewed impetus to the traditional radical elements among the students and university intellectuals, and fired the imagination of the growing band of educated young men who were just starting their careers in the armed forces. These were youths who, under a system instituted by Haile Selassie prior to the 1960 revolt, had been creamed off the senior grades in the high schools and drafted into the army, and in particular into the extremely high standard Military Academy at Harar. By 1974, these same young men were scattered throughout the army, mainly with the rank of major.

One of Haile Selassie's greatest aims was to complete the unification of Ethiopia, which entailed particularly the return of Eritrea to the fold.

The Italians, as mentioned earlier, had failed in their bid to conquer Ethiopia and in 1886 had signed a treaty with Menelik II, leaving them in control of Eritrea. Under Mussolini, they again began to cast envious eyes on the Empire of Haile Selassie, and in 1934, ignoring a Treaty of Friendship signed between the two leaders six years previously, Italian troops engaged the Ethiopian army in battle about eighty miles inside Ethiopia. Despite an impassioned plea by Haile Selassie to the League of Nations, Europe's leaders – preoccupied with their own fears of an impending war in Europe – allowed the Italian dictator to over-run Ethiopia.

The occupation lasted from 1936 to 1940, when, with the help of the British and other Allied governments, Haile Selassie – who had fled to Britain – returned to Ethiopia. At first the British – who, over the next few years, gave considerable aid to Ethiopia, training the police and army and advising the Emperor on legal and government structures – kept control of the former Italian colony of Eritrea. In 1952, however, on the advice of the United Nations, the

15

British reluctantly released their hold on the territory, and it became federated to Ethiopia, retaining its own National Assembly and a considerable degree of autonomy. In 1962 Haile Selassie unilaterally annexed the territory, making it an integral province of Ethiopia. Immediately hundreds of Eritreans left the country, many of them to emerge shortly afterwards as leaders of the various liberation movements whose joint action in the opening weeks of 1975 was to plunge Ethiopia into civil war. Their fervour for independence over the years was fired by frequent brutal acts against the civilian population by the Ethiopian Army, and by the harsh treatment meted out to the province by the Haile Selassie government in a succession of measures which deprived it of the fruits of its internal economic stability.

Haile Selassie's image abroad, however, remained that of a progressive reformer, and in an Africa desperately looking for a world figure to lead its emerging nations, his suggestions for a 'United Nations' of Africa fell on willing ears. In 1963 he presided over the inauguration of the Organization of African Unity, which set up its headquarters in Addis Ababa.

But it is easy to be harsh on the progressive who became an arch-reactionary. Haile Selassie was a victim of his background. In mediaeval times he *would* have been a great reforming monarch. In the twentieth century he was an anachronism. His biggest misfortune was being born too late and living too long.

His system of government naturally did not always attract altruistic administration, and as Haile Selassie declined in years he was probably less and less aware of what was going on around him. This is thought to be particularly true of the drought and famine in Wollo in 1973, which left more than 100,000 dead.

The masses, of course, had never owed real allegiance to anyone except their immediate king or Ras, and the image of an Emperor beloved by a united Ethiopia was a myth created by Haile Selassie and fostered by a few influential friends in the West, especially in Britain.

Haile Selassie became a megalomaniac; he *was* Ethiopia. Thus whatever system of government existed on paper, in reality all

16

power came from the Emperor, and under his rule, Ethiopia, beneath a mantle of modernity, had really changed little by the end of 1973. There were still serious tribal differences. In particular, Eritrea was kept firmly under military control; the Gallas in the south had much of their land taken from them by Amhara nobles; and Moslems everywhere felt they were being treated as rather less than second class citizens.

It is against this backcloth of tribal and religious rivalries, palace upheavals, mutual distrust and in-fighting by the nobles and provincial rulers, and the 3000-year struggle for survival against outside influences that the revolution of 1974 and its disintegration into civil war must be seen. But to bring the picture into sharper focus, it is equally important to look at Ethiopia as a country, at how it was governed, at the people and their living conditions and at the contrasts between the rulers and the ruled in the closing years of Haile Selassie's reign as absolute monarch.

3 Mud Huts and Mercedes

A not uncommon sight in Addis Ababa in the halcyon days of the Emperor was that of Haile Selassie handing out dollar bills to his poorer subjects in the market places.

A much less publicized activity under the Haile Selassie regime used often to take place in the streets of Addis Ababa in the eerily beautiful light of the city's spectacular dawns. Large canvas-sided police trucks would leave the depots scattered about the city, and spread out along the few main roads. Occasionally they would stop, a few para-military police would jump out and kick a bundle lying in the gutter or ditch at the side of the road. The bundle would stir, unfold itself from the filthy, smelly rags that passed for the only clothing it possessed, and become recognizable as one of the Ethiopian capital's innumerable beggars.

More police would be rounding up the street urchins, and the trucks would take their cargo of human flotsam to special compounds well out of sight of the casual traveller, where they might be kept for perhaps several days. This routine was performed prior to any visit to Addis Ababa by important foreigners. After all, such blatant poverty could not be allowed to tarnish the image of Haile Selassie.

However, as soon as the visitor to Ethiopia leaves the international airport on the south-eastern outskirts of Addis Ababa and travels along the wide, tree-lined dual carriageway towards the city centre, he is immediately struck by the contrasts. Cheek by jowl with the luxurious and often impressively designed modern homes of ambassadors, diplomats, and the Ethiopian aristocracy and senior military and government figures, are the floorless, mud and dung, tin, or turf-roofed huts – huddled together and intersected by dirt tracks – of the average Ethiopian citizen. Some of the better-off dwellings have a thin coating of plaster over the mud, and may even have a coat of white emulsion.

On the pavements – where such exist (most streets, even in the capital, have nothing more than a dirt path at either side) – sit the beggars. There, too, the street boys beg and the hawkers crowd round anyone resembling a visitor, trying to sell him brass crosses, Colobus monkey skins (an illegal trade), nylons, cassette tapes and chewing gum. Men relieve themselves openly wherever the need takes them, and women squat in the ditches, their modesty protected, more by accident than design, by their long, full skirts.

There are some modern shops and department stores, but they cater exclusively to the foreigner and the wealthy Ethiopian. The majority of the citizens make their purchases either in the vast Mercato – an enormous bazaar which is reputedly the biggest market place in Africa and which is at once fascinating and frightening for the tourist – or in small 'souks' (roadside kiosks).

Families tend to be large, and work is scarce. Much of the employment consists of service in the homes of diplomatic staff, foreign businessmen and other expatriate residents, as maids, cooks, gardeners and *sebanyas* – the guards that are needed day and night on every Western-style home because of the prevalence of theft. The average wage in the country is only £35 a year, and away from the main cities there is little employment other than on the land.

It is also a country where ninety-seven per cent of the people are illiterate, where seventy per cent have no recognizable form of employment. Where diseases like hepatitis, typhoid, smallpox and tuberculosis are endemic, and frequently epidemic. Where most people live in the most primitive conditions, scratching their existence from soil that is tired and eroded, and drinking water that is contaminated with every intestinal parasite known to medical science and a few that aren't.

19

Meanwhile vast areas of good land and forests remain untouched because wealthy owners are too busy investing abroad the wealth gleaned from other vast holdings. Indeed, the absence of any comprehensive and scientific approach to agriculture on a national scale, and particularly the almost total lack of any land conservation policy, was a major contributing factor to the extent of the famine which followed the severe drought conditions of 1972/73.

If Haile Selassie had fully maintained his status as a feudal Emperor, the masses might have continued to bear their lot with resignation. But in his initially genuine efforts to introduce reforms, then, later, in his desire to impress the developed countries with his progressiveness, he gradually provided the country with a series of constitutions and set up an administrative system which was to prove his undoing. The constitutions were not, in fact, worth the paper they were written on.

The Chamber of Deputies, or Lower House of Parliament, while elected after a fashion – by onhy a minority of the population – was powerless, because it could do nothing without the approval of the Senate or Upper House, whose members were appointed by the Emperor. And the nominal government, or Council of Ministers, was also appointed by the Emperor, and was answerable only to him, and not in any sense to either House of Parliament. The real government was the Emperor, who had to approve every bill and act of the legislative. And to help him decide, he had his Crown Council – a group of key people drawn mainly from the aristocracy who, equally, were answerable to no one but the Emperor. Above the Crown Council were the Emperor's personal advisers, many of them close friends from childhood.

Such a system was obviously inefficient and ineffective. But it was more. With so many people at so many levels having varying degrees of power, and being responsible only to the Emperor, it was also a recipe for corruption.

Had Haile Selassie been a man of unshakable integrity, he might have been able to keep the system free of graft. But he himself used either force or, more usually, bribery – in the form of cash, lands or positions – to get what he wanted, and many of the men around him took their cue from the top. Thus over the years vice and corruption in top places became the rule rather than the exception. 'You had to be corrupt to work for Haile Selassie,' one of his ex-favourites once told me. 'If you were honest he had no time for you.' That may be somewhat overstating the case. But the truth is that by the end of 1973 corruption was on such a vast scale that nothing short of a revolution could clean it up.

The extent of the moral and financial corruption in Ethiopia was nowhere more evidenced than in the tragic drought and famine in Wollo province in 1973 which was to prove a crucial emotional factor in the eventual overthrow of Haile Selassie. The seriousness of the drought and famine was first suppressed by the local administrators, and such reports as were sent to the central government in Addis Ababa were sat on. When foreign journalists exposed the extent of the tragedy, they were officially denounced by the authorities.

However, the same system of government which had produced this corruption also gave Ethiopia what the country had never had – a professional class, consisting of teachers, clerks, civil servants and office and factory workers in the many foreign-owned businesses that had sprung up and which were paying, by Ethiopian standards, fantastic wages. It also included, significantly, the junior officer ranks in the armed services. Such people had modest stone-built homes, instead of the mud-and-dung huts. A few had small cars. They could afford to shop in the stores where the wealthy Ethiopians and diplomats and foreign businessmen shopped. They could afford, occasionally, to eat at one of the many excellent restaurants in towns like Addis Ababa and Asmara. They were educated. They were articulate – and they had incentives. They could appreciate that the vast gap between the rich elite and the poverty-stricken masses was not an act of God, but the deliberate policy of men. And, in their eyes, of one man in particular.

It was a situation ripe for a revolution.

4 Ethiopia Deflowered

The Yekatit Riots (January 1, 1974 – February 26)

There had been rumours, but then, in Addis Ababa, there were always rumours. A long-time diplomatic resident has dubbed it 'the city of rumours – where every rumour is true'. Even so, in January 1974, with Christmas just over, few people paid much attention to gossip of a possible strike in the air force at Debre Zeit. It was said to be over pay, rising prices and internal disciplinary injustices.

A much more substantial rumour had filtered up to the capital from the deep south of the country. Soldiers at a camp near Negele, not far from the Kenyan border, had turned on their officers, arrested them, and taken control of the area. The well in the main barracks had dried up, and senior officers had refused to let the troops draw water from their own dwindling well.

Meanwhile, there was growing discontent in all sectors of the urban community over rising prices. Taking its toll of Ethiopia at the beginning of 1974, as of most countries, was the price of oil. The people who felt the pinch most were the emerging middle classes.

The teachers and the armed forces had other causes for complaint. The teachers' main concern was the Educational Sector Review – a proposed reform of the educational system which they felt was badly planned, and was being foisted on them without consultation by people who were out of touch with the realities of life in Ethiopia. The major cause of discontent in the armed services – especially the regular army and the air force – was, apart from pay, internal injustice. Senior officers – as in the case of the Fourth Division base at Negele – were accused of abusing their position, and in the crudest ways. There were complaints that soldiers were being ordered to help build extensions to officers' homes, landscape their gardens, clean their cars and even polish their 'civvy' shoes.

While all this discontent was simmering, the government announced a staggering fifty per cent increase in the price of petrol. That was bad enough. But the price rise, it was said, was part of a fiddle by elements in the government. Possibly sensing the unusually militant and discontented mood of the country, some members of the Lower House of Parliament demanded an investigation. This group was led by a non-active army major, Admassie Zeleke, the representative from Harar.

Under pressure from this Parliamentary group, the Commerce Minister, Ketema Yifru, admitted the increase in fuel prices was not entirely justified by higher crude oil prices. The oil refinery at Assab was not producing enough oil to pay for itself. And to make up the deficit, the government had come up with the idea of boosting the price increase on petrol. Parliament was sceptical, to say the least, and demanded the presence of the Prime Minister. (It was one of the quaintnesses of the Ethiopian Parliamentary system – at least to those used to Western democracies – that the Prime Minister and the other ministers had no right of speech, or even attendance, at sessions of the Lower House unless specifically invited.)

Aklilu Habte Wold, a man who treated his colleagues – and indeed his duties – in a cavalier fashion, secure, as he thought, in his closeness to the Emperor, ignored the MPs' demand. And, of course, there was nothing the MP's could do about it.

By the end of the second week in February – the first week of the Ethiopian month of Yekatit – the teachers in the secondary schools had exhausted their patience over pay and the Educational Sector Review. They announced that from Monday, February 18 they would strike, and advised parents not to send their children to school.

Students in Addis Ababa had traditionally been a source of

trouble for the Ethiopian establishment, and knowing of the discontent of their teachers, they were building up to what looked like one of their periodic outbursts.

Pupils at the Tafari Makonnen and Haile Selassie I high schools took the lead on Thursday, February 14 by attacking buses and cars passing their schools. Most Ethiopians carry a weapon — usually a pistol; indeed, there are estimated to be more arms per head of the civilian population in Ethiopia than in any other country in the world. So when stones began to hit private cars, some Ethiopian drivers retaliated by firing on the school children. At least one teenager was killed — and this naturally inflamed the rioters even more. Police moved in, and there was more shooting and several children were wounded, mainly in the legs.

On Friday, February 15 some of the left-wing groups in the university joined the high school pupils and there was sporadic rioting and clashes with police in various parts of the city.

The student voice was the voice of the nation's conscience — and the Haile Selassie regime had often tried to silence it with the most brutal methods. On this occasion, as usual, the city's tough riot police had been put on the alert, and on the afternoon of Friday, February 15 groups of these police toured secondary schools warning the pupils to behave.

At one school, however, the warning took a most brutal and sadistic form. A group of riot police took five pupils out of a classroom and played a vicious form of Russian roulette with them, making the pupils roll down a hill while the police fired at them. Three were killed, the other two badly wounded. By the time the teachers' strike started on Monday, therefore, the students were in an ugly mood. The Emperor returned to Addis from Eritrea to find his capital torn by scores of incidents and clashes at various schools between students and police.

The following day, Tuesday, February 19, the streets of Addis Ababa were unusually quiet. The caravans of donkeys and heavily-laden men and women heading for the Mercato were noticeably thinner.

Unlike the other expatriate schools, the English School, built on

24

the stiff-upper-lip, military traditions of its benefactors and patrons, stayed open. A gang of youths overpowered the guards at the school gate and stoned the nearest classrooms. Inside were nearly eighty children aged between five and seven. As the windows facing the road were smashed in, the screaming, terrified infants dived under their desks, while their young women teachers did their best to keep order and protect them. Many of the children were cut and bruised by glass and stones. On others the effect was psychological – and more lasting. My own then six-year-old son was one of several who had to have tranquillizers to help them sleep for weeks after.

Later that Tuesday the taxi drivers announced they were going on strike. With petrol suddenly increased from 50 to 95 cents a litre, they had an unarguable case for raising their prices. The government, however, had categorically refused to allow them to up the fares.

Many observers firmly believed the government would step in at the last minute and do something to take the heat out of this, and the other inflammable situations – for one very good reason. The city was full of African and European diplomats attending a meeting of the Organization of African Unity to discuss the OAU relationship with the European Economic Community. And even more VIPs were arriving daily for the OAU Council of Ministers meeting due to start the following Wednesday, February 27. The administration, however, seemed to be in a state of shock and did nothing.

The morning of Wednesday, February 20 saw more sporadic demonstrations by the students. But by lunchtime, they had linked up with the disgruntled and striking taxi drivers and had began stoning the buses of the Anbassa Bus Company – in which the Emperor and his family had the major stake. It was a traditional target for student outrage; for the taxi men it was a protest at the refusal of the bus drivers to support their strike. At first the demonstrators around the main roads in the city centre confined themselves to stoning buses. But, as I was among the first to find out, they soon turned their attention to anything on wheels. I had been attending the OAU meeting with the BBC's Andrew Walker and a resident American journalist, and we were heading out to my home on the southern outskirts of the city for lunch. Within a few hundred yards of Africa Hall, a crowd had gathered across the street, sullen, silent – and with fistfuls of stones. 'They don't look too friendly,' said Andrew. It was to prove a considerable understatement. We dodged round some side streets, hoping to come out ahead of them. Instead, we ran into another mob wreaking havoc on a stationary bus. We made another quick turn down a side street back towards the main road, hoping to be ahead of the first crowd. As we turned into the main road, with the second mob now blocking our retreat, we saw ahead of us, as far as the eye could see, thousands of people on either side of the tree-lined dual carriageway that leads to Mexico Square, a major junction about half a mile away. There was nothing else to do but go forward.

It was just our luck that, a short distance away, a bus full of passengers, with many of its windows already smashed, turned into the road ahead of us. The crowd, which so far had been still, erupted into action. The rocks began to fly. I shouted to the others to get down below window level, and put my foot hard on the accelerator and headed straight for the section of the crowd ahead which by now was beginning to close in behind the bus and chase it. Some rocks were also coming our way. Miraculously, we got through the crowd and past the bus and didn't stop till we were inside my home compound.

Because we were living in a rather exposed house between two army barracks, and not inside the large and well-guarded compound of Radio Voice of the Gospel, I had asked for, and been given, one of RVOG's armed guards as extra protection for the house and to ride 'shotgun' – quite literally – in the car with me in the evenings.

Andrew Walker had been visiting my home on the Wednesday evening, and at about 10.30 we set off for the Ghion Hotel near the city centre, where he was staying – complete with armed *sebanya* riding shotgun. The streets were uncannily deserted. Mine was the only car on the road, and after dropping Andrew off, the guard came in front beside me, rolled down the window, and rested the rifle on the ledge. As we drove along Ras Makonnen Avenue, the main north-south road through the city centre, a large black

American car swung out of a side street, right across our path. And suddenly, as the four men inside began shouting at me, I realized there were guns pointing out of the windows. But my *sebanya* had already seen them. He snapped out of his greatcoat cocoon and fired. It was more than the would-be hold-up men had bargained for. When I could get my heart out of my mouth, I muttered '*Igzer yistillin*' (thank you) to the *sebanya*. He just grinned.

The situation was rapidly disintegrating into anarchy. As the disturbances continued, it became increasingly obvious that the government would soon have to act. On the Thursday night they did. In a broadcast on the government – owned Radio Ethiopia, they announced that the army had been given full authority to deal with the situation. It was also announced that the government had decided to suspend the Educational Sector Review. The most important development, however, was the ordering of the troops onto the streets – which meant the NCOs and other ranks had a full issue of weapons and ammunition.

Throughout Friday and Saturday sporadic rioting continued, and few people ventured out.

For those two days in Addis Ababa, almost all activity – other than that of the demonstrators and the security forces – came to a complete halt. Except in the Grand Palace, where there was feverish activity.

The Grand Palace was Haile Selassie's office, and for two days it was the scene of unprecedented meetings. The Emperor met first with his Council of Ministers and listened as the Prime Minister, the Education Minister and the Minister of the Interior outlined the violence and disruption that was spreading outwards from the capital.

When faced with opposition, give them money, had been Haile Selassie's policy. On such premises a policy was devised to mollify the teachers and the taxi drivers, to appease the disgruntled masses and to keep the military dissidents quiet. Satisfied that handing out largesse would solve the problem, Emperor Haile Selassie brought the two days of meetings to an end and happily left Ras Asrate Kassa, President of the Crown Council and a former governor of

Eritrea, and Lt. General Abiye Abebe, President of the Senate, to work out the details.

So confident was he that on Saturday morning, February 23, he gave orders that he should be driven in his familiar maroon Mercedes into the heart of the seething Mercato district, where he went on a 'walkabout'. Immediately, the tension in the area which had followed the week's violence dispersed. 'Long live the Emperor,' cried his loyal subjects as usual. Some were heard to add, however, in the Emperor's hearing: 'But we don't care about the others.' Then it was announced that on Saturday evening the Emperor would make a nationwide radio and TV broadcast.

This turned out to be a rambling speech, full of rhetoric and platitudes. He appealed to the teachers to resume their duties and promised to study their grievances, including their pay claim.

Then came the crucial announcement. The price of petrol would be reduced 'as much as possible' and price controls were to be set on basic essentials, whether locally made or imported. The Emperor concluded by expressing his sorrow at the violence and damage caused by the rioting, and warning that 'strict measures' would be taken against those disrupting the peace. After his speech the Minister of Commerce, Ketema Yifru, announced that petrol would be reduced to 75 cents a litre, with immediate effect. In other words, the increase had been almost halved.

The following morning, Sunday, it was announced that the armed forces would also receive a pay rise, to take immediate effect, and ranging upwards from 18 Ethiopian dollars a month, bringing the basic rate for a private up to almost 100 dollars (about £20) a month – a good wage by Ethiopian standards, but less than was being demanded. The same morning, the government newspaper, *The Ethiopian Herald*, announced the toll of the week's violence:

> *Casualties* – 3 dead, 22 wounded.
> *Damage* – 75 buses, 36 private cars, 26 government vehicles, 7 diplomatic cars, 38 houses, 2 trains, 1 motorcycle.

The announcement also disclosed that nearly a thousand people had been arrested, including 350 armed taxi drivers, and charged with attacking the police. Seasoned observers of the Ethiopian scene drew the conclusion that if these were the official figures, then the real figures were likely to be at least double.

The effect of the Emperor's broadcast, however, did little to remove the tension. And although few people knew about it at the time, there was good cause for the general apprehension. It had been Haile Selassie's habit for years, on Sunday afternoons, to visit a school for the blind, of which he was patron and chief benefactor, a few miles to the south of the city. On Sunday, February 24 he made the same journey. But he made one stop first – to an army barracks on the Jimma Road, about a mile inside the city limits. A few hours before his visit, junior officers and other ranks had taken some senior officers hostage. Their complaints were, again, disciplinary injustices, corruption on the part of the senior officers, and not enough pay. After the Emperor had had a brief chat and made an appeal to the soldiers, the officers were released and an investigation promised.

Monday was tense but quiet. By mid morning, it looked as if the troops had the situation under control. The demonstrators had disappeared, and a few buses began to appear on the streets again. Because all now seemed well, Andrew Walker left for another assignment in Brussels. His plane took off from Haile Selassie I international airport at 6.30 am on Tuesday, February 26. It was due to stop over at Asmara, capital of the northern province of Eritrea, but it didn't land there – and it wasn't till Andrew arrived in Brussels that he learned why.

Shortly after his plane had left Addis Ababa, junior officers and other ranks of the Ethiopian Army's Second Division, based in Asmara, raided the quarters of their senior officers, and without a shot being fired, arrested them.

The Creeping Coup had begun.

'Asmara Takes Commanding Lead' (February 26–27)

John Talbot, the veteran Reuters correspondent based in Addis Ababa, was the first journalist to get the news from a contact in

Asmara. At about half past ten he got word that junior officers, joined by other ranks, had confined their officers – including the CO, Major-General Seyoum Gedle Giorghis – to their quarters. They had set up blocks on all roads leading into the city, closed the international airport, the banks, and the telecommunications centre. But they could do nothing about the microwave telephone link with Addis Ababa, short of blowing up the installation. So, by a series of telephone calls, we were able to piece the story together.

As at Negele, Debre Zeit and the various barracks in Addis Ababa, there had been a history of discontent in the ranks of the Second Division in Asmara, mainly over pay, but also over treatment by their senior officers. The 18-dollar increase announced by Haile Selassie at the weekend had not satisfied them. They wanted more – and regarded themselves as a special case because they were, as they put it, in the front line of the struggle against the Eritrean Liberation Front, the seccessionist guerilas who had been fighting for twelve years for the independence of Eritrea.

Soldiers had entered the palace of the Provincial Governor, Lt.-General Debebe Haile Mariam, and politely informed him he was under house arrest until further notice. That evening, troops burst into the government-owned radio station in Asmara, took it over and broadcast a list of twenty-four demands, which, they said, had been sent in telegram form to Addis Ababa. The demands included improved pension and injury benefits, better food allowances, improved housing arrangements, and, of course, more pay.

Late on the Tuesday evening, Radio Ethiopia in Addis Ababa announced that the Emperor had authorized a delegation to make the 450-mile trip to Asmara the following day to negotiate with the troops. Ironically, that Tuesday's edition of the English-language *Ethiopian Herald* had carried the headline: 'Asmara Takes Commanding Lead'. It referred in fact to football league tables but was all too appropriate in quite another sphere!

Wednesday, February 27 was an even more eventful day. When the government delegation – led by General Assefa Ayene, the Army Chief of Staff – reached the Second Division headquarters in

Asmara, all but Lt.-General Assefa Demissie, the Emperor's senior ADC, were detained as hostages.

At 7 pm Radio Asmara broadcast that General Assefa Demissie and a group of rebel officers had returned to Addis to put the mutineers' case to the government and the Emperor. Throughout the day the mutiny had spread to other units of the armed forces, and indeed into Addis Ababa itself. First the air force at Debre Zeit, then various army units in Addis Ababa – the Signals Corps, the Musicians, the Engineers and Transport Sections – had openly joined the rebellion by arresting their senior officers.

At the Red Sea base near Massawa, the Ethiopian navy had also joined in the spreading mutiny. The Deputy Commander of the navy (Haile Selassie was the nominal Commander) was Rear Admiral Eskinder Desta, grandson of the Emperor. Middle ranking officers, supported by ratings, politely informed the Rear Admiral that he wouldn't be going anywhere for a while.

However, with the help of some members of the household, he escaped to the harbour where, with some loyal officers, he took over a deserted naval vessel, cast off, and fled into the Red Sea. Within an hour, Eskinder Desta found himself in an even more embarrasing position for a Rear Admiral. His vessel had run out of fuel! He was eventually rescued by a French frigate and was later put ashore at Djibouti where he was to remain, unheard of and largely forgotten, for several months.

Meanwhile, early on the morning of February 27 Haile Selassie had ordered his generals to stage-manage a 'loyalty' demonstration in the grounds of the Palace. By noon, several hundred troops and police were assembled. The Emperor came out onto the balcony and addressed them.

It was a remarkable and electrifying speech in which the Emperor appealed to the soldiers to accept the pay rise offered, explaining, as he had done in his message to the troops in Asmara, that the country couldn't afford any more.

As Commander-in-Chief of the Armed Forces, he then told the men of all the services to obey orders. 'Enemies of the country are trying to divide Ethiopia,' he informed the troops. 'I call on you to

31

follow the example of your heroic fathers, who shed their blood to hand down a heritage of unity.'

After speaking in similarly emotional tones for about four minutes, the Emperor appeared to break down. As his voice broke and faltered someone led the assembled soldiers in a chorus of cheers and shouts of 'Long live the Emperor'. But it was a hollow occasion, and there was to be little to cheer about before the day was over.

Haile Selassie, however, flushed with success, then threw his security men into dismay by insisting on being driven around parts of the city, stopping and chatting to passers-by. It was a typical gesture of a man who was nothing if not a showman.

And the show had to go on. Shortly after the broadcast, ignoring the spreading anarchy within the military and the lack of any positive effects from his speech, as unit followed unit in locking up its officers, Haile Selassie moved across the road from his residential quarters – the Jubilee Palace – into Africa Hall to formally open the OAU Council of Ministers meeting. The atmosphere was electric. But the little man maintained his usual dignity – although people close to him noticed signs of strain which, even considering his eighty-one years, was unusual for Haile Selassie. His speech made no reference to the local situation.

After the formal opening ceremony, Haile Selassie went straight back into a meeting with his own Council of Ministers and members of the Crown Council, who had meantime decided that there was no alternative but to accede to the pay demands of the Second Division rebels in Asmara, giving a scale of between 90 and 150 dollars a month, improved allowances and better pensions. General Deresse Dubale was sent off to try to negotiate a similar deal with the troops in revolt in Addis Ababa.

It was about this time that the city of rumours was to produce its pièce de résistance. The whisper went round the Council of Ministers that the soldiers didn't just want pay rises, they were demanding that the cabinet be dismissed. It was true, of course, though at that time *no* formal demand had been made. Someone in the cabinet, however, knew it was coming. Perhaps significantly, one member of the cabinet was missing from this meeting: Lij (roughly translated as 'The Honourable') Endalkatchew Makonnen, Minister of Posts.

At the height of this stage of the crisis, Haile Selassie excused himself and left to play host at a reception for the Foreign Ministers of the OAU, due to start at 5.30 pm. Fifteen minutes later, General Deresse burst into the crisis meeping in the Jubilee Palace with more bad news. The entire Fourth Division – the major infantry and artillery section of the army, based in Addis Ababa – had thrown in its lot with the Second Division and the other Addis-based units and had arrested all their senior officers. Half the country's militia was now in the hands of NCOs. He also had heard rumours that the troops were out to get rid of the cabinet. Prime Minister Aklilu Habte Wold, and his brother, Akale-Work Habte Wold, immediately proposed that the entire cabinet should resign, and Aklilu turned to Information Minister Dr Tesfaye Gebre-Egzy and instructed him to draw up a resignation statement.

When the Emperor was told of Aklilu's plan he was far from pleased. Why should the cabinet resign? he asked. Was there some new demand from the military to this effect? Well, not exactly, said Aklilu. But there had been rumours. Even General Deresse had heard them.

Ras Asrate Kassa, President of the Crown Council, interrupted, angrily pointing out that no Ethiopian official ever resigned. If he failed in his post, he should be dismissed. It was virtually a demand that the Emperor should dismiss Aklilu, something which Ras Asrate and a number of others on the Crown Council had long dreamed of. Realizing this, Aklilu argued fiercely that although the antagonism might be directed against him personally, the criticisms affected the whole cabinet. One out – all out, was his view. (His apparent panic, however, was uncharacteristic: he was actually a very shrewd man – so shrewd in fact that he, alone probably, had read the signs, knew how serious his own situation was, and a few days before had quietly arranged for his French wife to fly out of the country and return to Paris. She did not return to Ethiopia.)

By the time the Council meeting broke up just after 7 pm a

statement had been agreed upon. It would say the cabinet had offered its resignation to the Emperor, who would let them know his decision shortly. The Foreign Minister, Dr. Minassie Haile, was meanwhile given the unenviable task of going back into the OAU reception and telling the assembled ministers that he could no longer guarantee their safety and that it might be wise if they postponed the rest of their meeting and left Addis Ababa.

At eight o'clock that night, Ethiopian Television News flatly announced that the entire 18-man government had resigned. Ethiopia was now a country without a government – and with NCOs running the bulk of its army.

Paper 'Rains' (February 28 – March 3)

The world awoke on the morning of Thursday, February 28 expecting news of a coup d'état in Ethiopia. All the elements were there: widespread rebellion in the armed forces following two weeks of public disorder; an entire government forced to resign because of demands by a group of NCOs; the great Emperor Haile Selassie humiliated in front of the assembled Foreign Ministers of his beloved African continent.

By mid-morning, more troops had appeared on the streets and taken up positions on public buildings. The offices and studios of Ethiopian radio and TV were occupied, as was the telecommunications building, troops had seized the international airport, and road blocks were springing up all around the city. Questioned about their purpose a young NCO explained: 'It's to stop any members of the old government from leaving the country.' The officer added that soldiers had in fact arrested a number of the ministers who had resigned, and were now looking for some of the others.

Thursday was also the beginning of the 'leaflet' revolution – what was to become a veritable 'little rain' of paper. From early morning, army helicopters had been flying low over the city. At lunchtime, they began dropping leaflets. The first of these was directed primarily at the service units and the police, who had so far not

34

committed themselves to the growing rebellion – most conspicuous among them being the Imperial Bodyguard, the army division with special responsibility for the protection of the Emperor and the royal household. It was a most unusual document, carefully worded to make it clear from the outset that the Emperor was not the target of their discontent. It also revealed that the authors – the Air Force, Airborne Division, 29th Brigade and Engineering and Signals sections – had refused to accept orders to go to Asmara to quell the revolt in the Second Division.

About an hour later another leaflet was dropped. This one was decidedly more political in content, using for the first time the phrase 'revolutionary movement', which, it said, had been started 'in search of the wolves who have of their own accord resigned'. The document demanded that the members of the ousted cabinet be questioned about their activities, and that land be returned to its rightful owners or to the government, and added: 'From now on, anyone given authority should be given it with the support of the popular voice and not by a limited class of people.'

Words – in particular on radio and TV – were to play a significant role in the whole revolutionary process, although so far the press had made no reference to what had been going on – a normal state of affairs under the Haile Selassie regime, which allowed nothing that could be construed as criticism of the establishment, no reference to any event or activity which did not have the blessing of the Emperor. An editorial in the Amharic language daily, *Addis Zemen,* urging support for the government, ended with the words: 'Ethiopia Tikdem' – which means 'Ethiopia First'. It wasn't until July, ironically, that the military movement began to make this the slogan or motto of their revolution, and it was emblazoned on posters, car stickers and lapel buttons all over the country.

The most significant events of that Thursday were going on indoors. Haile Selassie sent for General Abiye, Ras Asrate and the ex-Prime Minister, Aklilu. When Ketema Yifru and a number of other members of the ousted cabinet joined them shortly after 9 am they learned that the Emperor had asked General Abiye – one-time

35

husband of Haile Selassie's youngest daughter, Princess Tsehai – to form a government. Abiye and Ketema Yifru left for the Senate House, the General hastily to pick some key members of his new cabinet, Ketema to draft a speech for the Emperor announcing the new government. Ex-Premier Aklilu and some other members of the ex-Council of Ministers went off to the Cabinet Room in the Grand Palace to prepare a written reply to the Second Division mutineers.

Only Ras Asrate Kassa stayed behind with the Emperor. A quiet, dignified and brilliant man, Ras Asrate was as much a 'royal' as the Emperor; indeed, his father had at least as great a claim to the throne as Haile Selassie. Now the nobleman pulled no punches. He told the Emperor in no uncertain terms that another reshuffle of his favourite clique would not solve this problem. The mood of the people was against the whole idea of the old establishment and the revolt in the armed forces was not a cause, but a symptom of the problem facing the country.

'Suspend the constitution, dismiss Parliament, declare yourself Prime Minister and get to work on a new constitution,' Ras Asrate told him.

While Ras Asrate was trying to persuade the Emperor to adopt this bold course, other forces were at work. General Assefa Demissie had been continuing his negotiations with the rebellious army units in Addis Ababa, and during the past few days, one of the NCOs he had been talking to had carefully sown a seed in the General's mind. Why not let Lij Endalkatchew Makonnen, the Minister of Posts, run the government? The General was assured that this would be welcomed by the military. It was an idea that appealed to General Assefa. Lij Endalkatchew was a second cousin of Ras Asrate – and could also trace his ancestry to King Sahle Selassie.

Lij Endalkatchew was also the one cabinet member who had not been present at the crisis meeting when the rumour had come that the military wanted Aklilu and the cabinet to resign. And he was related – by marriage – to an Airborne Division Colonel, Alem-Zewd Tessema, a man whose name was to become prominent a few weeks later.

General Assefa returned to the Jubilee Palace just before lunchtime to discover that a press conference had already been set up at the old Grand Palace to announce General Abiye Abebe as Premier. Shortly afterwards, the pressmen and photographers were told, apologetically, that the conference had been cancelled. Instead, the Emperor – again without prior warning – went on Radio Ethiopia at 2 pm and named Endalkatchew as Premier, General Abiye Abebe as Defence Minister and Lt.-General Wolde-Selassie Bereke as Commander of the Armed Forces. He also issued a general warning that public peace and security should not be disturbed, and announced a new pay structure for the army.

On Friday morning, March 1, Endalkatchew hurriedly arranged a press conference in his old office in the Post Office building on Churchill Avenue. The students had also planned a major demonstration that morning and, uncharacteristically, police and troops, instead of dispersing them, had allowed a crowd of about 5,000 to mass in Arat Kilo near the university, and had then shepherded them as they marched round the city.

At the head of the march was a group of students carrying an effigy of ex-Premier Aklilu with a noose round its neck, with placards demanding that he be hanged. Just as Endalkatchew was starting his press conference the demonstrators reached the Post Office building and stopped outside, chanting 'Endalkatchew Out' and 'Death to Aklilu'.

Above the noise, the new Prime Minister pledged to govern justly, and to form a cabinet based on men of 'talent, youth and experience'. As he went on, the noise began to subside as the main body of demonstrators moved further down the road. Suddenly shots rang out. A group of demonstrators had apparently broken away from the main body and rushed part of the police cordon – more in jest than with hostility, according to bystanders. But a policeman panicked and instead of following orders to fire in the air, he fired into the group. It was the signal for a riot which ended with several arrests, about a dozen injured, and at least one student dead.

The Second Division in Asmara received a written reply to their demands, expressed their acceptance, and called on other units to end the rebellion. They were not in sympathy with the wider political demands of the Addis-based units, they said, and in particular were opposed to the radicalism of the air force. General Abiye used this information in negotiations with the Fourth Division, and obtained the release of the detained ministers in return for guaranteeing that no reprisals would be instituted against the rebels.

Saturday, March 2 was Adowa Day — a national public celebration to mark Emperor Menelik II's victory over the Italian invaders in 1896. The day was a symbol of freedom to Ethiopians, and observers waited with bated breath to see what it would bring. No one, however, was prepared for the first shock of the day. For when Emperor Haile Selassie made his traditional visit to take part in the special Thanksgiving Service in St. George's Cathedral, the man sharing the comfortable back seat in his maroon Mercedes — the place of honour normally taken by the Prime Minister — was not Lij Endalkatchew, but Aklilu Habte Wold. The new Premier wasn't even in the royal retinue. As the crowd round the church began to cheer the Emperor, they suddenly saw Aklilu. There was a break in the cheers, an audible gasp from hundreds of throats, and the cheering continued at considerably reduced volume. It was a tactical error — a rare one — on the part of the Emperor.

By Sunday, March 3 — outwardly a day of peace and near-normality, apart from the continuing troop patrols on the streets — what had started as a pay revolt was already developing into the hydra-headed monster that was to stalk the land from end to end in the months that followed. Still on top — but only just — was Emperor Haile Selassie and his circle of ministers, ex-ministers, aristocratic associates and aides, and military and government advisers, all desperately trying to maintain a status quo which assured them a life of luxury and privilege. Even this, however, was a house divided against itself, full of traditional rivalries, conflicting loyalties and intrigues. On the civilian front was a disgruntled urban population ripe for moulding into a revolutionary movement, under the leadership of left-wing students, intellectuals and university lecturers. And within the military, there were divisions between moderates and radicals. Quarrels were also about to develop between the civilian radicals and those in the military over whose revolution it was. Add to this ethnic rivalries, individual opportunism and greed, and the unpredictability of the massive rural population, and one begins to see why the next few months were to be called 'The Creeping Coup'. The radical elements were to emerge more and more as the dominant force. But the balance of power was to sway back and forth like a demented pendulum for some time before then.

On Sunday evening the 8 pm Amharic news on Radio Ethiopia began with the voice of Endalkatchew announcing his cabinet. Dejazmatch Zewde Gebre Selassie, great grandson of Emperor Yohannes and an Oxford-educated liberal reformer whose progressive views had brought him into many a skirmish with the establishment, was Minister of the Interior; Lij Michael Imru, radical son of another descendant of King Sahle Selassie, the 'Red Ras' Imru (so-called because of his socialist views and the fact that he had given most of his land to his peasant workers) was Minister of Commerce and Industry; General Assefa Ayene, who had been Army Chief of Staff and one of those held hostage by the Asmara rebels, was Minister of Civil Aviation (shortly switched to Minister of Posts); and Kifle Wodajo was a Minister in the PM's office.

'Speaking Out' (March 4-5)

Monday, March 4 started off quietly enough. The new cabinet was sworn in and the *Herald* carried an editorial headed 'Time for understanding' which was an Endalkatchew-inspired plea repeating the theme that the new government should be given a chance to tackle the many problems facing Ethiopia.

There had been a few helicopters buzzing low over the city centre around lunchtime, dropping more leaflets. They called for a government directly elected by the people, for freedom of the press, freedom of speech and redistribution of land.

The main units of the army in Addis Ababa issued a statement disassociating themselves from such leaflets. A message was also sent from Fourth Division headquarters to Debre Zeit warning the airmen that if they did not give up their arms, they would find themselves up against the army. It was enough to frighten most of the radicals into submission, although some of the key figures fled, to remain in hiding until the tide turned.

That afternoon brought one of the ugliest incidents in the story thus far, although only marginally connected with the mainstream of events. By this time the prisons were pretty full, and fullest of all was the main civil prison in Addis Ababa, Akaki jail — where conditions are appalling at the best of times.

A few minutes after four o'clock a diplomat friend who lived near the prison phoned to tell me that a riot was going on inside and that the guards were shooting in all directions. Hours later there was a brief official statement that there had been an attempted prison breakout and that the guards had been forced to open fire. The official toll was thirty-three dead. But several witnesses who watched, horrified, from the upper storeys of the OAU building nearby counted about a hundred bodies lying in the dusty courtyard.

Meanwhile, the message of widespread and growing opposition to the whole structure of the establishment was underlined from a new quarter — the Confederation of Ethiopian Labour Unions, CELU. This was an organization of only about 100,000, but the members held key skilled positions in industry and commerce. (Government employees were excluded, since they had no constitutional right to belong to any union.) Suddenly it found its courage and presented the new Endalkatchew government with a list of sixteen demands on behalf of the Ethiopian workers. And they threatened to call Ethiopia's first general strike, starting forty-eight hours later on the Thursday, unless their demands were met.

Endalkatchew realized that if he was to salvage his position he had to appear to be as keen on change as the next soldier, student or worker. Throughout that night he worked on his plan. Even as he worked, the government-owned *Ethiopian Herald* was preparing to

40

publish one of the most remarkable articles in its history.

It appeared as a front page editorial headlined 'Speaking Out', and was written by one of the two vice-ministers in the Ministry of Information, Tegegne Yetashework. 'We are now in a period of transition,' it began, 'Now is the time to speak out to make sure that the transition is not only a change of names and faces but mainly of concepts ... Some of the former ministers suffered from a malady they diagnosed as political insecurity and prescribed for themselves the amassing of wealth which has now called for a surgical operation.'

At 10 o'clock on the morning of Tuesday, March 5 Endalkatchew went to the Jubilee Palace to see the Emperor. Until then Haile Selassie had issued all his instructions to the new premier through the old one, Aklilu Habte Wold! The Emperor listened carefully as Endalkatchew outlined a programme of sweeping constitutional reforms. Half an hour later the Emperor had agreed in principle to the whole programme, and Endalkatchew was told to draft a statement to be broadcast later by Haile Selassie.

While he was doing this, he instructed the Information Ministry to alert the local and international press, and to announce on radio regularly throughout the rest of the day that the Emperor would make an important broadcast that evening.

The new cabinet had its first meeting that afternoon. A delegation from the Labour Unions was invited to meet them and discuss their demands, point by point, including one that government employees should be allowed to form unions and become part of CELU. The Unions Conderation also wanted greater safeguards in the event of strikes and the right to hold public meetings and recruit more members. The meeting lasted well into the night.

By 8 pm that Tuesday evening, however, there must have been few people who, if they had access to them, were not tuned into radio or TV for the Emperor's speech. In his archaic, classical Amharic, the Emperor said he had ordered a revision of the revised constitution of 1955 with a view to making the Prime Minister responsible to Parliament, and to guaranteeing greater civil rights. The Prime Minister was to convene a conference to undertake a study of the constitution and report back to him within six months. The new constitution would also reorganize and streamline the processes of justice and speed up the legal procedures.

As I wrote for the BBC that night: 'The first reaction was among the scores of newsmen who crowded the lobby of the Addis Hilton. Most of them seemed to think a lot of fuss was being made about very little. But experienced observers in the country say that for Emperor Haile Selassie to go even this far was dramatic enough by Ethiopian standards.' And so it was. The mere fact that the Premier was in future to be answerable to Parliament rather than the Emperor was a major departure from Haile Selassie's form of administration.

In the same despatch I added: 'But while leading Ethiopians recognize this as another major step in the relaxing of his grip on the country by the Emperor, leading possibly to some kind of constitutional monarchy, the people who have been doing most of the agitating – and presumably this could include those behind the military revolt and the threatened general strike – do not think the Emperor's statement goes far enough. And if anything, the carefully-couched language of the Emperor's statement, promising greater civil rights and an improvement in the method of government, can only encourage those elements who want once and for all to see an end to the almost feudal system by which Ethiopia has been ruled for generations.'

It was to be even more prophetic than I thought.

'Beautiful Ethiopia has been deflowered' (March 6-18)

The curfew had been lifted on Tuesday night, and by Wednesday, March 6 the army appeared to be releasing their grip on the capital. But when by Wednesday evening there was no word from CELU about calling off the strike, in spite of renewed government appeals, apprehension began to grow.

In fact the strike was almost total, but the day passed almost uneventfully. By mid morning thousands of workers had gathered outside the offices of CELU, near Mexico Square, for a mass meeting addressed by Confederation officials. Again troops and police were standing by in force; again there was no trouble.

The most remarkable event of the day, though, was an article in *The Ethiopian Herald,* written by Yacob Wolde Mariam, one of the more experienced journalists in the Ministry of Information. It began by asking the public's forgiveness for not reporting honestly in the past, went on to praise the Emperor, and concluded with an extraordinary appeal to Ethiopians not to do away with the monarchy — extraordinary since no one, publicly at least, had even remotely suggested anything of the kind! But the comment was historic, since to have made it a week or so before would have meant instant arrest for the writer, and probably also for the editor.

The general strike had originally been planned for only one day; but it lasted through Friday, Saturday and Sunday, and as negotiations continued between CELU leaders and the cabinet almost round the clock, the strike gained even more support.

On Sunday evening, March 10, however, Haile Selassie decided to intervene personally. He sent for the union leaders and the cabinet, listened to the demands and to the cabinet's replies, and got both sides to agree. But later on Sunday night they sent word to the cabinet that there were further demands — government employees should be allowed to form ujions, and there should be no reprisals against strikers and no wage cuts without union consultation.

It took all of Monday to sort out these demands, and the general strike was not officially called off until late on Monday night. By this time two more strikes had started — oje involving several hundred workers at the Tobacco Monopoly, and a considerably more serious one by employees of the Civil Aviation Authority. In both cases pay was only part of the problem. Staff were demanding the removal of senior management figures whom they accused of corruption and mismanagement. It was to be the beginning of a wave of such demands from workers in all sections of industry, commerce and in government departments.

That Monday, too, Emperor Haile Selassie gave a rare press conference — it was to be his last, in fact. As we waited to go in, we watched members of the ousted and supposedly disgraced Aklilu cabinet strutting round the grounds, standing in clusters beside the Emperor's caged lions, and being shown the usual deference by the Palace staff. Pith-helmeted veteran members of the elite Palace contingent of the Imperial Bodyguard lent their unique dignity to the ancient Menelik Palace and its well-kept grounds, and it was from one of these, a distinguished-looking, middle-aged Sergeant who had spent a lifetime in the royal household, that an Amharic-speaking American colleague, Bill Lee, got what was to be a prophetic comment. Why, Bill asked him, were all the old ministers continuing to wander around the Palace as if they were still running the country, and commanding the same obsequious service from the scores of flunkies on the Emperor's staff?

'As far as the Emperor is concerned,' replied the Sergeant, 'they *are* still running the country.' Then he added, with startling and daring candour: 'But the Emperor is making a mistake. And he'll pay for it. They're all going to end up in jail – and so will the Emperor if he's not careful. They'll drag him down with them.'

Haile Selassie's office was a cross between a Victorian drawing-room and the showroom of a junk-dealer. The collected bric-à-brac of a dozen foreign tours littered the walls and every surface. The Emperor sat at his huge, ornate desk, his five-foot two-inch frame encased in one of his heavily be-ribboned military uniforms.

In his soft, rather gravelly voice, Haile Selassie indicated his desire to see more power devolve on Parliament and the people. He also expressed his willingness to consider allowing the creation of political parties. Up till then the press conference had been held in muted tones. But on this point of political parties the Emperor became more animated, and produced a rare spark of humour, winning polite laughter from the journalists when, using the royal 'we', he said: 'We don't really like the idea of political parties. We think one party is good enough for Ethiopia. As it is, there are as many political parties in Ethiopia as there are members of Parliament!'

But, he went on – and it was obvious that here he would brook no argument – the monarchy was the unifying force in the country

It always had been, and it always would be.

On Thursday, March 14 the Council of Ministers had a four-hour meeting with the teachers' representatives, and on Saturday it was announced that adjustments and increments had been approved – although somewhat lower than the teachers had demanded.

This period also produced a lighter moment when a demand was presented to the Ethiopian Orthodox Church Patriarch, Abune (Holy Father) Tewoflos, by five hundred priests and rural clergy. They too, wanted more pay – and would go on strike unless it was forthcoming. Their document said wages for the 'low clergy' – the travelling priests – were between 3 and 8 dollars (approximately 60p to £1.40) a month, while the 'privileged' clergy in the churches got 15 dollars (£3) a month. It also attacked the hierarchy of the church 'who have betrayed their vows towards God' and denounced their 'exploitation of land and farmers'.

The significance of the episode is that it helps to throw some light on why, in Haile Selassie's last days as Emperor, he was to fail so miserably to rally the support of the church hierarchy, and particularly of the Abune Tewoflos. For although the church was to remain strong in the central provinces – as an institution – its leadership had long since been discredited, both inside and outside the church.

Press freedom continued, however, and on Saturday, March 16, *Addis Zemen* carried a hard-hitting attack on the old cabinet: 'When men, women and children were dying in their tens of thousands in Wollo as a result of famine, it was inexcusable for the former government to hide the facts from the Ethiopian people.'

It was the first direct attack on the Aklilu government in relation to the drought, and it lit yet another fuse of anger which was to smoulder over the next few months and then be fanned into flame in the weeks preceding the Emperor's overthrow.

The most remarkable article of the whole period came, again, from the pen of Vice Information Minister Tegegne Yetashework. It contained a remark that was to sum up the schizophrenic attitude of many educated urban Ethiopians like himself – who wanted, out of genuine desire or self-preservation, to go along with the reform movement, but who also regretted the passing of the era of good times for the few. 'Beautiful Ethiopia has been deflowered and she is never again going to be intact. The changes at the top have not affected the lives of the masses at the bottom.'

However the real significance of articles such as this, and those of Yacob Wolde Mariam, was that the state of the country and its future had become a matter for open, public debate, on a scale never imagined in the wildest dreams of the hitherto underground radicals. That was really the single most important achievement of what became known as the 'February Revolt' period of the Creeping Coup.

The combined effect of the Yekatit Riots and the army pay mutinies gave the country's radicals an opportunity to take the initiative. It also opened the way, for the first time since the 1960 coup attempt, for those deliberately created divisions in the artistocracy and military to come to the surface. And it forced the Emperor to appear at least to be giving up his almost god-like hold over the nation.

Most of all, it wrested control of the media from the establishment, and left them free to be used by the forces which opposed the regime. And they were to use them superbly.

Before then, however, Ethiopia was to experience three months of outward confusion and fierce behind-the-scenes conflict.

5 The Demented Pendulum

The Split Widens (March 19–30)

To use a saying from British weather-lore, March had come in like a lion, and it looked like going out like a lamb. To all outward appearances, the strikes — apart from the Civil Aviation Workers' dispute — were over, and if the newly-awakened Confederation of Ethiopian Labour Unions, CELU, was snapping at the heels of some employers it had not dared to confront before, that was only to be expected in the country's new political climate. The teachers were back at work, the cabinet was getting to grips, at least in theory, with the country's problems, and most significant of all the armed forces appeared to have settled down.

However, in the middle of this relative peace and tranquillity I came into possession of a document which purported to be a 'Message from the armed forces to the people of Ethiopia', and expressed considerable doubt as to the intentions of the new government genuinely to implement reforms. The aims of its authors were to bring the members of the old cabinet to justice — in courts presided over by the military; to have several of the newly-named members of the Constitutional Commission replaced; and to investigate members of the new cabinet 'to find out if any of them are misdoers' (sic). It added that the military were 'determined to struggle' for the implementation of their aims.

One of the barometers of impending military activity in Addis Ababa was to be the appearance of armed, battle-dressed troops at the compound of Radio Voice of the Gospel and inside the studios of Ethiopian Radio and TV. When, on the morning of Monday, March 25, two truck-loads of troops arrived at RVOG, we knew something was going on. (In the early days we were never quite sure whose side the troops were on, but after June they were clearly acting on the orders of the radicals.) On this occasion it was the first swing of the pendulum *against* the radicals. During the night twenty-five junior army officers who had played leading roles in the revolt had been arrested by troops loyal to the Defence Minister, General Abiye, and the Airborne Division had been sent to Debre Zeit to surround the air force base.

That night a statement was read in the name of the Emperor announcing that he had ordered investigations into allegations that 'members of the present and former governments had accumulated wealth illegally or misappropriated government property'. A special commission was being set up which would 'separate the guilty from the innocent and bring the guilty to justice'.

Next morning, Tuesday, the Commissioner of Police in Asmara, Major-General Gashew Kebede, was having a meeting in his office with General Seyoum Gedle Giorghis, the Commander of the Army Second Division, when a group of army and police NCOs burst in and arrested them. The NCOs then took over Radio Asmara and broadcast a list of six demands, among them that *all* senior civil and military leaders in Asmara should be arrested and brought to court on charges of corruption. They also demanded the immediate re-establishment of communications between 'The Armed Forces of the North' – as they described themselves – and the air force base at Debre Zeit.

That evening, radio and TV programmes in Addis were interrupted for a statement from the armed forces. It affirmed loyalty to the Emperor, pledged support for the new government, and said the proposed Commission of Inquiry into Corruption should be given a chance. And it attacked 'certain factions using the name of the armed forces to spread propaganda', and acting 'in the guise of false patriotism'.

On Wednesday morning, March 27, the Asmara rebels sent the

Provincial Governor, Lt.-General Debebe Haile Mariam — whom they had detained — to Addis to present their demands to the government. Later, assured that their demands had been accepted in principle, the Asmara mutineers announced on Radio Asmara that they had released the Police Commissioner and the Second Division Commander, and allowed the international airport — which they had seized on Tuesday morning — to re-open.

Endalkatchew had been finding his position untenable. He certainly didn't have the confidence of the country. He didn't have the wholehearted support of the cabinet. But, worst of all for a man in his position under the Ethiopian system, he had scarcely any access to the Emperor. Haile Selassie was still consulting Aklilu Habte Wold as if the ex-Premier was still in office!

Beneath these tensions, however, there had developed a scenario of which Machiavelli would have been proud. There had been no plot before the February Revolt to overthrow the government or the Emperor. But there had quickly developed a whole network of plots. The first one had been a rather ad hoc affair — and had been instantly successful. That was the rumour that the military wanted to get rid of Aklilu. How the rumour was started may never be known. But it is clear who took advantage of it — Ras Asrate, General Abiye and Lij Endalkatchew. It is doubtful that they were working together at this stage. But each of them had strong incentives to move against Aklilu. Ras Asrate and General Abiye suspected — with justification — that Aklilu was actively working against them, trying to undermine their position with the Emperor. Aklilu had for some time been playing on the Emperor's natural distrust of those close to him, and since Haile Selassie revelled in, and actually encouraged, such situations — as part of his method of survival — Aklilu had found a willing listener.

But there was a very special reason for the Emperor's distrust of Ras Asrate. The Ras was the one man whose blood line was at least as royal as Haile Selassie's, who might upset the Emperor's plans to keep the throne in his family name.

Endalkatchew was, on the other hand, just an ambitious man who

49

seemed willing to serve the interests of any group which would help him achieve political power.

Thus, out of those initially unintegrated moves to oust Aklilu, there had emerged a loose-knit 'triumvirate' determined to maintain the conservative structure of Ethiopian society, but in a way which would serve their own ends. In general terms, in the months to come, Ras Asrate would provide the brains, General Abiye the brawn, and Lij Endalkatchew would be the malleable front man going through the motions of seeking to establish a new society.

To further complicate matters, a number of senior military men, a key figure among whom was Lt.-General Assefa Ayene, former Air Force Commander and now Minister of Posts and Telecommunications, were planning ways in which they could use the unrest in the armed services to their own advantage.

On Friday, March 29 a helicopter owned by the Canadian Can-West Aviation Company and operated on behalf of the American Tenneco Oil Company, had taken off from Asmara to fly to Massawa on the coast. The helicopter failed to arrive, and its burned-out wreckage was found just inland from Massawa. It was assumed it had gone down in a violent storm in the area that morning. But there was no sign of any of the five men who had been aboard. Villagers questioned near the scene said they had been taken away by 'bandits' – the popular euphemism for secessionist guerillas of the Eritrean Liberation Front, the ELF.

Within the previous week, in fact, there had been renewed ELF activity, the most significant being an attack on the country's only copper mine – a joint Ethio-Japanese project – on which high hopes for the economy had been placed.

'An administration rotten to the heart' (March 30)
On Saturday, March 30, Prime Minister Endalkatchew, rallying from his despondency and threat of resignation, announced the names of the Anti-Corruption Inquiry Commission, and again appealed for time. But the public was impatient, and the general reaction was summed up in a leading article on the front page of

50

The Ethiopian Herald that day, claiming that the Inquiry Commission proposal raised 'more questions than answers'. It was feared it would be a body without teeth, aimed only at nibbling at the edges of corruption and ignoring the 'big fish'.

One reason for this fear was the composition of the Commission. There was widespread criticism that some of its members were mere puppets of the government. Another cause for apprehension was the extent of the corruption. This was rammed home in another *Herald* article by Yacob Wolde Mariam, who said 'The Ethiopian administration is not only rotten to the heart but also riddled with corruption.'

On that same Saturday the Prime Minister formally opened the Constitutional Conference and told its members that their main concern should be to clarify the redistribution of power. In reply, the Antiquities Minister, Tekle-Tsadik Mewkria, said bluntly that many of the upheavals in Ethiopian history would never have happened if the monarchical system had been founded on a constitutional base. It was essential, he said, for independent legislative, executive and judiciary powers to be written into the new constitution.

Recognizing the pressures that were building up, particularly over the Corruption Commission, Lij Endalkatchew that night made a forty-five minute radio and TV broadcast to the nation. Looking relaxed and in control, he said the members of the Commission had been chosen for their integrity and honesty. But if any questions arose, he would be prepared to 'make adjustments'. In fact, he said, he was prepared to face the Commission himself if necessary.

He then went on to outline the contents of a forthcoming statement of policy which, he said, would be in the form of the country's first White Paper (after the British system) and would include a specific section on land reform. It would also make provision for all government and industrial workers to have the right to strike – a right hitherto enjoyed only by members of CELU. But he warned that the current wave of strikes (the aviation workers were the main group still out) was illegal.

51

He ended with another appeal to the armed forces and the public for law and order – and a promise of 'open government'.

The Great Air Force Bomb Plot Fiasco (March 24 – April 8)

The following evening the Defence Minister, General Abiye Abebe, dramatically announced that there had been a plot to overthrow the government, led by 'irresponsible individuals using the name of the armed forces'. The plot had been discovered in time, he said, and he categorically denied that it had involved any members of the armed forces. Some of the plotters had been arrested, but General Abiye warned that there were still people at large who had been involved and were continuing their attempts to disrupt the country.

Two of the people he was talking about had, in fact, contacted me the previous Wednesday, and in cloak-and-dagger fashion, involving changes of cars and secret signals, we had arranged a meeting that afternoon. General Abiye had been wrong about there being no armed forces involvement. They were both in the air force – one a leading aircraftman, the other an NCO. But that wasn't the only 'inaccuracy' in the General's statement.

There had never been a plot to overthrow the government. What had happened was that the 'ginger group' of radicals in the air force – of which the NCO claimed to be the leader – had, with the support of officers and pilots at Ethiopia's three main air force bases and of similar radicals in several army units, decided to do something to show their dissatisfaction with the speed of reforms. The plan was to 'buzz' Addis Ababa with a squadron of jet fighters, while colleagues in the Airborne Division dropped leaflets from helicopters. The Asmara units would do the same, and the action was planned for Monday, March 25.

At two o'clock that morning, however, truck-loads of troops from the Airborne Division and armoured vehicles from the Tank Division in Addis had burst into the air force HQ compound, and been deployed across the runways to prevent any planes taking off. Other troops had surrounded the airfield perimeter fence. There had been a brief skirmish, during which my informants had escaped.

The two men had then prepared and were about to circulate a document refuting three allegations: that the air force's 'committee' of radicals (similar committees had been formed in most units by this time) were working with foreign agents; that they had intended to bomb Addis Ababa; and that they had set mines around the air force HQ. (This last accusation was patently untrue in view of the ease with which the Airborne and Tank units had been able to enter the base.)

Now, said my informants, they had turned the whole situation against the government and sent General Abiye an ultimatum that unless their demands were met, and the troops withdrawn, Ethiopia would remain without any air defences.

In the few days which followed my encounter with the two airmen, I was able to piece together how their plan had come unstuck.

It transpired that, not surprisingly, the radical air force committee had in it a 'fifth columnist' who had reported the planned buzzing and leaflet drop to someone he knew to be interested in hearing about such things on behalf of the government: Colonel Alem-Zewd. The Colonel had informed Endalkatchew. The Premier was under pressure from conservative members of the regime to take a harder line against extremist elements, and particularly those in the air force, an acknowledged hotbed of radicalism. But Endalkatchew was afraid that any firm action undertaken without a definite excuse would backfire and have the effect of uniting the opposition. Colonel Alem-Zewd's information gave him the excuse. Between them, they hatched a plot to turn the situation to their advantage.

A rumour was spread that 'foreign agents' had infiltrated the country and were planning to overthrow the government. The air force, it was understood, would cooperate with the enemy agents.

This wasn't an entirely implausible story. Everyone knew that a high percentage of the air force was Eritrean. Everyone knew that Arab countries, particularly Libya, supported the ELF. And with the recent turmoil, a Libyan-backed, Eritrean-led coup was just within the bounds of possibility.

On Sunday, March 24 Colonel Alem-Zewd called a meeting of the Airborne and Tank Divisions in a hangar at the Army Aviation Base on the Jimma Road in Addis Ababa. He revealed that he had uncovered a plot involving the air force, and that he had been instructed to ask their help in thwarting it.

All that General Abiye's announcement of the foiled plot achieved was to add to the tension and unrest which was continuing in spite of the Premier's appeals. In fact, about the only good news that week as far as the government was concerned was that the Civil Aviation workers ended their stike.

Endalkatchew now seemed trapped in a vicious circle. He needed a period of respite from civil and military unrest to get on with reforms, and he needed the reforms in order to appease those who were creating the unrest.

Premier v. Parliament (April 8 – 14)

The cabinet were, for the most part, genuinely trying to initiate what, in their eyes, and considering their sheltered elitist background, were genuine reforms. And the document the Prime Minister presented to the nation on the evening of April 8 as his White Paper outlining the policy of the new Council of Ministers was, in the Ethiopian context, remarkably progressive.

The government's first priority, it said, would be to deal with the drought and the financial situation. It would also give every assistance to the commission set up to make Ethiopia a constitutional monarchy.

The document, which was a kind of 'legal revolution' as important as the military one which had made it possible, then went on to outline the government's plans for the creation of a fairer society.

But it was on the subject of land reform that the policy document appeared most revolutionary. It said no one should be allowed to own more land than he could develop, and that any excess should be taken away and given to people who wanted to work it. There was to be legislation to prevent the widespread practice of absentee landlords claiming government grants and not using them for agricultural purposes. The government also planned to return to public ownership the vast sections of forest land now in the hands of private individuals.

Two other clauses seemed even more pointedly aimed at the very heart of the old regime — and caused some eye-brow raising in diplomatic circles. One said a special office would be set up to deal with citizen's complaints, in the manner of an ombudsman. The other said that in future the Ministry of the Interior would be responsible for the provincial governors. Until then, both duties had been the jealously-guarded personal prerogative of the Emperor.

It had not gone far enough, however, to stem the growing reform movement.

The Chamber of Deputies (the elected Lower House of Parliament) and the Senate (the Imperially-appointed Upper House) had scheduled a joint session on the drought for April 10. It was to be an historic occasion: for the first time in Ethiopian history, the Prime Minister — who constitutionally had no right of address in Parliament — was to address a joint session. His brief was to speak about the drought.

Endalkatchew had other ideas, however. He intended to take advantage of the presence of Ethiopian radio and TV and the foreign media to expound on his White Paper. When the time came for one of the Senators to propose that the Premier address the joint session on the drought, the Senate President Bitwoded (a title meaning 'Beloved') Zewde Gebre Hiwot, who was chairing the meeting, gave the floor to another Senator, who invited the Premier to speak on the subject of the new cabinet's policy statement.

Immediately there was uproar. Desks were banged, papers and abuse hurled across the chamber by a vocal group of MPs. The session broke up without the Prime Minister even being allowed into the chamber, but with the agreement that a seven-man joint committee would be set up to 'consider under what conditions the Prime Minister might be permitted to address a joint session of Parliament'.

The same day demonstrations by city council employees forced

55

the resignation of the mayor of Addis Ababa, and workers' allegations against senior officials in the state-run electricity, water and telecommunications industries were threatening to bring about more strikes. There were also strikes going on among non-medical hospital workers and court officials in Asmara. The nation was becoming 'strike happy', in fact, as workers in both the public and private sectors, so long deprived of any kind of rights of industrial action, took advantage of the new era of apparent freedom.

Emperor Haile Selassie was sufficiently realistic to recognize that one day soon Ethiopia would be without him, and now took steps to settle the delicate question of his successor and avert the internecine conflict among the nobility which many both within and outside Ethiopia had predicted would follow Haile Selassie's death or removal.

The heir to the throne, Crown Prince Asfa Wossen Haile Selassie, had never fully recovered from a stroke suffered in January 1973, and was still convalescing in Geneva, with little sign that he would ever return to Ethiopia, much less be fit to become monarch.

The Crown Council were expected to intervene at some point and exercise their power to declare the Crown Prince incapable of the throne, and name another successor. Haile Selassie decided to take the initiative and when more than seven hundred dignitaries gathered in the huge reception hall at the Grand Palace on the evening of April 14 to give their Emperor Easter greetings, he dropped his bombshell.

The heir-apparent, to succeed the ailing Asfa Wossen, would be the Crown Prince's only son, Prince Zera Yacob Asfa Wossen, then a 20-year-old student at Exeter College, Oxford. The news was greeted with an emotional display of cheers and tears.

'The brink of disaster' (April 15-25)

The day after the succession announcement, Prime Minister Endalkatchew brought the nation back to earth with another nationwide radio and TV broadcast. The latest wave of strikes and industrial and civil unrest, he said, had combined to confront the country with grave internal economic problems. Ethiopia, he warned, was now 'on the brink of disaster'.

But the chief topic of conversation was speculation about what might happen the following Saturday, April 20, when the country's Moslem community planned to stage a massive demonstration. It was widely feared that it would precipitate a violent clash between religious groups who were traditional enemies.

Early on that Saturday morning, thousands of heavily-armed police and troops took up positions along the proposed demonstration route. Conservatively it was thought that around 30,000 actually took part in the march, and that tens of thousands lined the route.

Crowds at the roadside often clapped and cheered the carefully marshalled marchers as they passed, especially when they expressed anti-establishment sentiments. Indeed, it was not so much a pro-Moslem demonstration as a massive show of public solidarity against the establishment. The day passed without a single incident requiring the intervention of the police and the troops. The only people outwardly displeased were the capital's Orthodox Christian priests, who demanded the right to stage a counter-demonstration the following Monday. It was an almost total flop.

In an attempt to keep the armed forces and police militants in check, Endalkatchew had been making a series of visits to a number of barracks and police stations, addressing massed gatherings of the men. The police especially were showing signs of restiveness, and complained of being treated with less consideration than the army. And police in the north had sent a message to the government demanding the removal of the country's police chief, Lt.-General Yilma Shibeshi.

One of the biggest rallies addressed by Endalkatchew was of 2,000 men at the army's Fourth Division headquarters. When he invited questions at the end of his speech, several soldiers and young NCOs told the Prime Minister bluntly that they knew the former ministers, led by Aklilu, were 'interfering' in the running of the country and trying to delay reform. If Endalkatchew didn't do something about this, the soldiers would 'take necessary steps to ensure that these suspect people do not escape justice'.

The following day, Friday, April 19, the demands of the soldiers and of the student demonstrations found formalized, legal expression in the Chamber of Deputies, where a resolution was passed recommending that members of the old cabinet be placed under house arrest. The Premier knew, of course, that he was not the man to approach the Emperor and demand Aklilu's arrest. Endalkatchew and Haile Selassie were still barely on speaking terms. But a direct demand from the military ... It was time to call in Colonel Alem-Zewd again.

The Colonel, now Commander of the Airborne Division, had, in fact, emerged as the leading member of a joint services committee of army and air force militants. It had been formed, as an extension of the original group which had staged the February Revolt, to ensure that promised reforms were carried out.

On Monday, April 22 he and a Junior Aircraftman, Girma Fisseha, led a delegation to the Emperor and, after expressing their loyalty, demanded 'in the name of the armed forces' that he order the arrest of the former cabinet ministers. Haile Selassie refused.

There then followed four days of confusion, both public and behind the scenes, unparallelled in the revolution before or afterwards. Exactly who did what on whose instructions may never be fully known, since so many of the principal actors in the drama are now dead. But from a wide variety of independent (and remarkably consistent) sources, there emerged a picture of plot and counter-plot overlapping and interweaving, and of a tangled web of intrigue and double-cross fused by events into a single course of action that was to prove decisive.

When Colonel Alem-Zewd reported back to Endalkatchew the Emperor's refusal to order the arrest of Aklilu, it was realized that somehow the armed forces must get into a stronger position vis-à-vis the Emperor in order to force the issue. Events generally were getting out of hand, so Endalkatchew did what Aklilu had done in February when faced with near anarchy: he advised that the military be called in.

Not all of the cabinet favoured the idea of allowing too much power to get into in the army's hands. But on the Tuesday morning, the Prime Minister was given more justification for his proposed course of action. Eight hundred postal workers began an indefinite stoppage, and telecommunications staff threatened a strike from the following Sunday unless they were allowed to form a union. Government printers also threatened a strike. Existing rail and transport strikes in Addis, Asmara, Massawa, Assab and Dire Dawa were causing shortages of imported goods and holding up vital exports. And there were sporadic public and student demonstrations. That evening the government issued a stern warning. Strikes and demonstrations were illegal and were leading the country towards 'anarchy and confusion'. Strikers must return to work and permission would have to be obtained for marches and demonstrations. To enforce this, the security forces had been placed on alert to deal with civil and industrial disobedience and unrest.

The tone of the government statement was verging on a declaration of a state of emergency. And there was a genuine crisis. The widespread indignation and unrest in the armed forces was being fanned by inflammatory propaganda spread mainly by students and university radicals, and the groups of workers not affiliated to CELU were being actively helped and encouraged by the Labour Confederation.

The situation was also ripe for other kinds of exploitation, and among the military, the students and the workers were professional agitators planted by Aklilu Habte Wold, who hoped through disruption to discredit Endalkatchew's government and force its resignation as a preparation for his own return to power.

However, Aklilu also had to get rid of some of his highly-placed enemies, especially those in the senior echelons of the police and armed forces. Fortunately for him, many of these were the same men who were already unpopular with the rank and file soldiers and police. Accordingly, Aklilu had also placed his agents within the army and police ready to raise a hue and cry against any particular general.

Meanwhile, Colonel Alem-Zewd was trying to consolidate his

position as a leader of the revolution within the armed forces, and, because of this, was being pressed by the more radical elements and by Aklilu's agents to include police and army top brass in any list of people to be datained.

In the face of so much natural and organized opposition, the Prime Minister's Tuesday night warning was like a red rag to a bull. Wednesday erupted into violence: schools, taxis, and government buildings were stoned; there were several shooting incidents; and two thousand Highway Authority workers joined the spreading strikes.

The order was given for the security forces to act. On Thursday morning, April 25, troops appeared on the streets, took up positions at key installations and patrolled in jeeps. Nevertheless, the day passed surprisingly uneventfully.

What neither Haile Selassie, Endalkatchew, nor Aklilu knew was that their destinies were already in the hands of a group of men who had been waiting for just such an opportunity for years. They were aware of Endalkatchew's schemes regarding Aklilu, and for reasons of their own shared his aim. They were also aware of Aklilu's plots against the police and army generals, and since it suited their purposes, they were willing to go along with these too. These men were to have a profound influence on the events of the next forty-eight hours — and beyond.

6 Brinkmanship

Arrests and Confrontation (April 26-28)
On the morning of Friday, April 26, the Emperor agreed to receive
another delegation from the armed forces. As Endalkatchew stood
silently in the background, the delegates again demanded the arrest
of the Aklilu cabinet. Again the Emperor refused. The soldiers
decided it was time to take the law into their own hands.

Units were sent first of all to surround the homes of the
ex-ministers. But as word of what was happening spread, a number
of generals raced for the palace hoping to seek refuge, like Aklilu,
with the Emperor. One of the first generals to be arrested was the
Commander of the Imperial Bodyguard. In the ensuing confusion,
the Bodyguard offered no resistance when Fourth Division soldiers
entered the Palace and demanded that Aklilu and the senior military
men who were hiding inside be handed over. Eyewitnesses in other
parts of the city saw senior police officers being marched out of their
offices with their hands on their heads.

Late that evening, an armed forces broadcast on radio and TV said
that 'acting on their own initiative' they had arrested all the
members of the former cabinet. They had also detained the recently
sacked police chief, Yilma Shibeshi, the ousted ex-mayor of Addis
Ababa, and the governor of the National Bank. In addition –
although this was not publicly disclosed at the time – they had
detained almost two hundred generals and other senior officers in
the armed forces, air force and the police throughout the country.

61

The situation had all the makings of a fully-fledged coup, but a statement at 8 am the following morning, Saturday, appeared to dispel this notion. Issued in the name of 'The Imperial Bodyguard, the Fourth Division, the Police, the Air Force, the Territorial Army, and in collaboration with the Second and Third Divisions,' it said that 'by order of His Imperial Majesty' the former cabinet had been 'put into one place until justice [was] done'. It concluded that the new cabinet should be allowed to go ahead, and warned that the security forces would now deal with the 'few trouble-makers in the civilian population' who had been creating disturbances.

It seems that under the influence of Colonel Alem-Zewd, the real radicals were prepared, for the time being, to go along with the myth of supporting the government. The Colonel, however, was consumed with ambition; he was enjoying his position too much to jeopardize it by putting too restraining a hand on the military committee, which that day began systematically working its way through a list of five hundred other key figures in the civil and military authorities who would have to be 'neutralized' in the interest of reforms.

One might have expected Endalkatchew, or at least Defence Minister General Abiye Abebe, tk make some comment. Instead it was Colonel Alem-Zewd, as chairman of what was now styled the 'Armed Forces Committee', and Jr. Aircraftman Girma, who called a press conference at Fourth Divison HQ to explain what they had done. They also took the opportunity to issue a warning against 'strikes and unnecessary demonstrations' – a portent of things to come.

Industrial Relations – Army Style (April 29 – May 1)
Ethiopia emerged from that weekend of intensive military activity with the country in the grip of widespread industrial unrest. State-employed electricity, water and telecommunications workers were to strike from Tuesday, April 30 in defiance of government warnings. The dockers' strike at Massawa and Assab had ended, but the busmen and railwaymen were still out, and municipal workers

in Asmara walked out on Monday morning demanding the removal of the city's mayor.

Late in the evening of Monday, April 29, the government issued a final warning and appeal to the telecommunications staff – whose strike was regarded as the most serious since it would effectively cut Ethiopia off from the outside world. Endalkatchew said that anyone who struck would be fired, and announced the setting up of a joint committee of government officials, police and security forces under the Ministry of Defence to co-ordinate and ensure the implementation of the government'a directives.

This National Security Commission (NSC) as it was called, was in fact a quite separate creation of the Defence Minister, General Abiye, set up with the dual aim of coping, by force, with the deteriorating civil and industrial situation, and of giving the administration its own military 'wing' to counteract the radical Armed Forces Committee.

That Monday night I and several other journalists were in the telecommunications office filing what we assumed to be our last messages for some time, and anxious to get them out before the strike started at midnight. With only a few minutes to go to the deadline, the clatter of the teleprinters was suddenly drowned by the sound of heavy vehicles rumbling to a halt outside. A dozen or so soldiers in full battle kit burst into the room, and through the open door we could see more troops spreading out through the building.

We correspondents were eventually allowed to go, after assuring the soldiers that our messages had been sent, but the staff on duty in the building – including about twenty telephonists manning the international exchange – were kept there all night. It took the armed forces most of the following day to round up the rest of the staff and forcibly bring them to work, but twenty-four hours and about forty arrests later, the telecommunications strike was over.

This rough and ready lesson in industrial relations set the tone; the following morning, April 30, two jeep-loads of troops screamed to a halt outside the headquarters of the Labour Confederation, CELU, and eyewitnesses saw several union officials being bundled unceremoniously into the jeeps. Shortly afterwards the Ministry of

Defence (suggesting the action had been taken by the newly-formed NSC) issued a warning that CELU would be closed down unless it stopped agitating and encouraging strikes. This show of force persuaded many of the other government employees on strike to start drifting back to work.

Late that Tuesday evening it was announced that Lt.-General Assefa Ayene had been arrested by the armed forces and relieved of his position as Minister of Posts, following allegations from the Second Division in Asmara that in a previous post as Commander of the Ground Forces, the General had plotted to destroy dissident troops in Asmara.

The main area of conflict, however, now existed between the military and the civilians, and Ethiopia celebrated May Day with a warning from CELU that if the NSC tried to close them down, they would call another general strike. The continuing presence of heavily armed troops at the telecommunications office, the electricity station, the waterworks, the bus depots and government offices was a deterrent to strikes, but the question was, as an Ethiopian friend put it, 'How long can you keep a nation at work with a gun in its back?'

The Defectors (May 1-27)

Within the cabinet there were serious disagreements developing. The Minister of Agriculture, Bulcha Demeksa, had already quit his post and returned to his Washington job with the World Bank, and Belai Abbai, a former Land Reform Minister, had never actually taken up his appointment as ministerial representative to the European Economic Commission. Some ministers were particularly unhappy with the creation of the NSC and wondered, with some justification, if there was any point in the continued existence of the cabinet.

Unhappiest and most uncomfortable of all was Dr Minassie Haile, the Foreign Minister carried over in the same post from the Aklilu cabinet. On May 8, after threatening to do so since March, he finally quit.

Monuments to past glory: an Ethiopian couple in national costume stand amid the Castles of Gondar, built in the ancient capital of Ethiopia with the help of the Portuguese in the 16th century.

Mediaeval monarch: Emperor Haile Selassie, Elect of God, King of Kings, Conquering Lion of the Tribe of Judah, absolute ruler of Ethiopia for almost half a century – ousted by a 'bunch of upstart young soldiers'. Born too late and lived too long.

Imperial guardians: one of Haile Selassie's pet cheetahs; in the background, a member of the Imperial Body Guard.

Victims of the 1973 Wollo drought disaster.

ቍጥር   ዘና

ነሐሴ 21 ቀን 1966 ዓ.ም

___አዲስ አበባ / ኢ ዜ አ / __   በኢትዮጵያ የሚገኘው የቢ.ቢ.ሲ. ሬዲዮ ጣቢያ

ወኪል የኢትዮጵያን አንዳነትና እርምጃ የሚያረን የተባለተ ዘና በማስተሳለፉ፟የመዉረሻ

ማስጠንቀቂያ የተሰጠው መሆኑን አንዱ የማስታወዪያ ሚኒስቴር ቃስ አቀባይ ዛሬ ማምሻዉን

አስታወቀ ::

3:30/ን. ḍ. ২.

AFP-184

ETHIOPIAN WARNING

ADDIS ABABA, AUG 27 (AFP).- THE ETHIOPIAN ARMED FORCES COORDINATING
COMMITTEE TODAY ISSUED A FINAL AND ''STRONG'' WARNING AGAINST THE
REPRESENTATIVE OF THE BRITISH BROADCASTING CORPORATION AGAINST
REPORTING ''UNFOUNDED'' FACTS BOUT ETHIOPIA.

  THE WARNING FOLLLOWED A B.B.C. BROAICAST ABOUT RESTRICTIONS
IMPOSED ON EMPEROR HAILE SELASSIE'S MOVEMENTS, OBSERVERS NOTED.

  WITHOUT SPECIFYING, THE COMMITTEE SAID THE BRITISH RADIO
STATION HAD REPORTED FALSE INFORMATION ABOUT ETHIOPIA. AFP
Ẅ22   20.13

*You have been warned!: The official Amharic press release by the Ethiopian News
Agency of a 'final warning' to the author over his coverage of events in Ethiopia for
the BBC. Below is the English version put out by the reporter for the French news
agency, AFP. Ironically, that reporter was expelled from Ethiopia in March 1975 for
his coverage of events. The author's warning was issued by the Haile Selassie regime,
the AFP expulsion by the military regime. Plus ça change, plus c'est la même chose!*

Experiment in power-sharing: Professor Mesfin Wolde Mariam, chairman of the Commission of Inquiry into Corruption, with his vice-chairman, Major Mersha Admassu, at the inaugural news conference in July 1974.

The puppet: Lt.-Gen. Teferi Bante, Chairman of the Provisional Military Administrative Council since November 1974. He is only nominally head of the government, and takes his orders from a group of army majors.

The triumvirate: (left to right) Major Mengistu Haile Mariam, Lt.-Gen. Teferi Bante and Major Atenafu Abate, Second Vice-Chairman of the PMAC, at the rally launching the National Work Campaign.

Say it with flowers: a tank – bedecked with flowers from well-wishers only hours after the announcement that Haile Selassie has been deposed – stands guard outside the National Palace in Addis Ababa.

Occupation or protection? The headquarters of Radio Voice of the Gospel. With only a few breaks, the station was 'occupied' by troops almost constantly from the outbreak of the February Revolt. Initially they were sent to protect the station.

The Zemecha: students on parade in Addis Ababa at the launching of the National Work Campaign on December 14 1974 pass the Ministry of Education. But for these students education has been suspended for a year while they go into the countryside to spread the message of Ethiopian socialism.

Monuments to present folly: (top) the Municipality, or City Hall, in Addis Ababa after a bomb explosion on December 3 1974; (bottom) the foyer of the Wabe Shebelle Hotel in Addis the same day. Both bombings were believed to be the work of the ELF, although the government officially blamed relatives of those executed on November 23. The military rulers admitted to 2 dead and 13 injured.

There was, of course, one other member of the former cabinet who had escaped arrest — Endalkatchew himself, who had been Minister of Posts under Aklilu. And there were some in the new administration who thought that the Prime Minister should follow Dr Minassie's example.

Endalkatchew's cabinet was disintegrating. Bulcha Demeksa's replacement as Agriculture Minister, Kassa Wolde-Mariam, had still to return from an extended visit to the United States. The Minister of Planning and Development, Tekalign Gedamu, had offered his resignation. Lij Michael Imru — originally appointed as Endalkatchew's Commerce Minister and then switched to the PM's office as Coordinator of Social and Economic Affairs — was returning to Geneva, where he had been Ethiopian representative to the UN Bureau, ostensibly to settle his affairs and bring his family back to Ethiopia. He was gone a long time.

Similarly, Information Minister Ahadu Saboure, who had been humiliated shortly after his appointment by outrageous and unfounded press attacks alleging corruption while he was ambassador in Somalia, was about to go to Djibouti 'for a few days' to clear up his affairs there. It was to be a long 'few days'.

Before his world began to collapse about him, however, Endalkatchew did have one moment of glory. On May 9 he finally succeeded in becoming the first Ethiopian Premier to address a joint session of the two Houses of Parliament.

And even as he was assuring everyone that the situation was now under control — with almost a third of his government either arrested, fled or quitting — one of the ablest men in the whole administration, Oxford-educated Dejazmatch Zewde Gebre Selassie, Minister of the Interior, was confiding in some friends that he was on the point of quitting, frustrated at finding his role completely usurped by the NSC and the Armed Forces Committee.

Unrealistic or not, at the end of his speech, Endalkatchew was given a standing ovation.

Parliament was the scene of considerable activity over the next week or two, as the Deputies urged measure after measure on the Endalkatchew administration. All the while, the Ethiopian press criticized and heckled them to such an extent that press coverage of Parliament became a subject for debate in itself.

The chief instigator of all this government-baiting was the Harar MP, Major Admassie Zeleke, who mounted quite a successful public investigation into the inefficiencies of the Assab oil refinery. Finally, on May 18 the Major announced that he was resigning as an MP in protest at 'the government's continued disregard for Parliament's decisions'. In fact he didn't resign – but the gesture brought him excellent publicity as a 'man of the people'. It wasn't the last time the Major was to hit the headlines.

On May 27 a group of armed men burst into the American Evangelical Mission hospital at Ghinda in Eritrea and attempted to kidnap two doctors. They failed, but took prisoner two nurses, one of whom was later found shot dead.   Behind this particular raid was the guerilla group who had captured the five Americans from the wrecked helicopter – one of whom, the pilot, had been taken ill and required urgent medical attention.

'They can't make us work' (May 27 – June 4)
The nation was still working 'with a gun in its back'. But one group of workers was rather less intimidated than might have been imagined.

This was the telecommunications staff, whose main grievance had been corruption in the higher levels of the Imperial Board of Telecommunications, IBTE. In particular, they wanted the removal of seven officials. Their strike committee had been arrested – and so had the seven officials – in the confrontation at the end of April. But within a week the officials had been released and were back at their desks.

The staff had met and formed a new action committee, and on May 8 had demanded that their colleagues be released and the officials removed. To press home their demand the employees staged a sit-in hunger strike. For the next two weeks staff and military played a cat and mouse game. Finally, on May 25 on the orders of the NSC, the twenty-four members of the *new* strike committee were arrested – some of them at home, others at the IBTE headquarters.

It took the telephonists, telex operators and other telecommunications staff two days to organize themselves again. But on May 27 they announced a total strike would start at midnight. It would also involve staff at the government radio stations, whose technicians came under the aegis of IBTE.

Once again it was the army and not the civilian government which conducted the negotiations. But after several hours of talks, the IBTE employees refused to back down. Troops again burst into the telex office late at night. This time it took a little longer for the correspondents to talk their way out.

The following morning, May 28, power and water authority workers came out in sympathy. The state radio stations were silent until mid-morning, when the army brought some technicians in at gunpoint and ordered them to work – or be shot.

Although limited services inside Ethiopia were maintained, international communications were completely cut off. One employee told me 'They may be able to make us stay in the building – but they can't make us work. Some of us would prefer to be shot.'

The dispute was to continue through most of June with frequent interruptions to the country's international communications, and was abandoned rather than resolved as the genuine military radicals on the Armed Forces Committee began slowly but surely to take control and thwart the activities of General Abiye's NSC.

Somali Interlude (June 4-19)

The Organization of African Unity was holding its Council of Ministers' meeting, followed by the Eleventh Heads of State Summit, in the Somali capital in mid-June and two questions concerned observers of the Ethiopian scene. Would Haile Selassie attend? And would the Ethiopian-Somali border dispute come up?

Any hopes of keeping the Ethiopian-Somali dispute out of the headlines at the Ministers sessions and the Summit were quickly dashed. In the impressive People's Hall in Mogadishu groups of

Somalis and exiled Ethiopians handed out leaflets to delegates, attacking Ethiopia over Eritrea and the 'occupied' territories of Somalia.

The Ethiopian delegates had been angered by the distribution of leaflets, but had decided to hold their temper. But when a book appeared on the official OAU bookstall – fiercely attacking Ethiopia, alleging atrocities and claiming she was planning a massive invasion of Somalia – it was too much.

The head of the Ethiopian delegation, newly-appointed Foreign Minister Dejazmatch Zewde Gebre Selassie, had returned briefly to Addis and it was left to the Vice Foreign Minister, Araya Ouqba-Egzy, to go into the Council Chamber in the People's Hall and accuse the Somalis of using the OAU meeting as a 'forum to launch a propaganda campaign against Ethiopia', and to draw attention away from Somalia's militaristic claims.

The 'pamphlet' war continued against Ethiopia, although when Haile Selassie arrived in Mogadishu he looked relaxed and composed. The huge form of Somali President Siad towered over the Emperor as he met him at the airport, but Haile Selassie's dignity seemed to put them on equal terms, and the two men smiled and chatted about the weather and the Emperor's flight from Addis.

But for some of us, the Emperor's coming was almost eclipsed by the arrival with him of someone who had last been heard of sitting ignominiously in the middle of the Red Sea in a fuel-less ship – Rear Admiral Eskinder Desta, grandson of Haile Selassie and erstwhile Commander of the Imperial Navy. He had slipped back into Ethiopia a week before, and had preferred to accompany the Emperor to Somalia rather than stay unprotected in Addis.

It was to be an unhappy few days for the Emperor. He was involved in a public exchange of words on the border dispute with Siad Barre at the opening session of the Summit, and had a lengthy and tough confrontation with him, first in front of the OAU's 'Good Offices' committee, and then in private. Attempts to get the two men to sign a non-aggression pact failed.

Haile Selassie left Mogadishu looking tired and defeated.

Before the OAU Summit ended, the Ethiopians were to be

subjected to further indignities as the Eritrean Liberation Front — who had a permanent office in Mogadishu only a mile from the Conference Hall — circulated a thick dossier to delegations, containing their case for Eritrean independence and indicating that they would take stronger action themselves unless the OAU supported their cause.

The OAU did not, of course — at least, not as a body. It couldn't very well support a secessionist movement against the country in whose capital it had its headquarters!

So the ELF set about implementing their threat.

The Storm before the Storm (June 20-27)

On June 20 the Eritrean guerilas struck the first blows in their intensified campaign. That afternoon an inter-city bus hit a landmine on the main road eighty miles south of Asmara. Eight passengers were killed and nineteen injured.

In the early evening Provincial Minister of State Ibrahim Khumed Arei — a member of the Eritrean Provincial Council and adviser to the Governor General of the Province — was shot dead at point-blank range when his car was stopped a few yards from his home in Asmara. He had been Secretary for Social Affairs in the former Eritrean Federal Assembly, but was regarded as having sold out to the central government in Addis. Later still, five policemen were ambushed and killed just outside the city.

Then, on June 22, the guerilas released the nurse kidnapped from the American mission hospital — but only after it had been agreed to give them medical supplies. A week later they also released the helicopter pilot, Don Wederfort, after holding him for fifteen weeks. But they said the other hostages would be put on trial on charges of 'exploiting the natural resources of Eritrea'.

The most decisive events were not going on in Etitrea, however, but in Addis Ababa and Debre Zeit. Throughout June the radical elements in the Armed Forces Committee had been organizing themselves, and as the month drew to its close, they began to move.

Colonel Alem-Zewd was still the nominal chairman of the

Committee, but the radicals, particularly in the air force – whose headquarters were still occupied by the Airborne Division – were pressing hard and openly for action. The first sign of this conflict in the military came on June 22 when there was a brief gunfight between some paratroopers of the Airborne Division and a group of airmen at Debre Zeit. One died and about nineteen were injured.

Colonel Alem-Zewd reported to the Prime Minister that his 'left wing' was getting out of hand with their demands for action to be taken to stop corrupt officials and relatives of the arrested ministers leaving the country and taking their money with them. So, on Thursday, June 25 Endalktchew announced that a complete ban on foreign travel for all Ethiopians – including ministers, government officials, the judiciary, members of semi-state organizations and MPs – was to take immediate effect. The only exceptions would be people travelling on official business for the government, and then only with prior approval. Furthermore, guarantees would have to be provided that they would return.

The following day, Major Admassie Zeleke – the Harar MP hailed as a champion of the people against the establishment – headed a delegation of eight MPs to the Fourth Division headquarters and addressed a mass rally of two thousand soldiers. Claiming to speak in the name of the Chamber of Deputies, he demanded that the military release twenty-five of the detained ministers, including Aklilu Habte Wold, the ex-Premier.

The Chamber erupted at this news. Next day all business was suspended while a stream of MPs hurled abuse at Major Admassie, who had calmly taken his place in the Chamber just after lunch. He was accused of bringing Parliament into disrepute with the people by his unilateral action. The row spilled over into the following day – Friday – when the Deputies voted to suspend Major Admassie and his group for a week.

But if the MPs were upset, the military was furious. As far as the radicals were concerned, this was the last straw.

7 Ethiopia Tikdem

The Purge Begins (June 27 – July 1)

The anger in the armed forces was quickly turned into action. While MPs were shouting hysterically across the Chamber at Major Admassie the day after his visit to Fourth Division HQ, the Armed Forces Committee was 'taken over' by the radicals, and, before he could be caught, Colonel Alem-Zewd fled into the countryside. The committee's new leaders sent a message through their senior obficers to General Abiye and the Prime Minister demanding stronger action against Major Admassie and his group.

Twenty-four hours later, on Friday, June 28, the Committee was informed that the Premier and Defence Minister had refused to do anything.

The Committee knew that the detention of the Aklilu cabinet and the few other officials rounded up at the end of April had only scratched the surface of the problem, that the real forces of resistance to reform were in the aristocracy, the Senate, the Crown Council, and around the Emperor. They were ready for the reply from Endalkatchew and General Abiye. Orders were immediately given for detachments of men from the Fourth Division, the Corps of Signals and the Engineers to occupy the premises of Radio Ethiopia, Ethiopian TV and Radio Voice of the Gospel.

Shortly afterwards I found myself sitting in one of the news studios at RVOG, with battle-dressed troops – rifles and sub-machine-guns in businesslike positions – facing me through the glass panel overlooking the master control room, as I read a hastily-translated statement brought into the station a few minutes before by an army captain, who demanded it be broadcast immediately.

The statement recapped on the activities of Major Admassie's group of MPs and the failure of the authorities to punish them. Then it went on: 'We, the armed forces, police and militia, would like to notify the public that we are ready to take the necessary action against the detained cabinet members and at the same time, would like to express our loyalty to the Emperor and the Ethiopian people at large. We also demand the cooperation of the public and will make further statements in due course.' The message of loyalty to the Emperor was not convincing.

Earlier that afternoon, the Prime Minister and the cabinet had been having a joint meeting with a number of Crown Councillors, including Ras Asrate Kassa. Soon after it started, a messenger came in and passed a note to the Defence Minister, General Abiye, who excused himself and left the meeting. At that moment jeep-loads of soldiers were being despatched to the homes of a number of prominent figures in the government and nobility, including General Abiye's. Someone in the army who knew what was about to happen had telephoned a warning to his home, and the General's wife had sent the message to the cabinet meeting. It was later claimed by members of some of the other families involved that the General had also been told to warn several other people, notably Ras Asrate Kassa.

The General appears to have made only one call – to Ras Mesfin Shileshi, one of the richest and most powerful nobles – before taking refuge in the back room of a shop owned by a Greek businessman on Addis Ababa's Piazza. From there he organized his escape into the countryside. Within an hour of his leaving the shop troops turned up, and finding their quarry gone, arrested the owner of the shop instead.

The armed forces had more success with some other arrests – notably ex-Foreign Minister Dr. Minassie Haile, Major Admassie, the Harar MP, Crown Councillor Yilma Deresse and a number of officials, including the influential administrator of Trinity Cathedral, the 'Canterbury' of the Ethiopian Orthodox Church.

The following morning, June 29, additional troops were sent to the radio stations, the banks and public buildings while others seized the international airport in Addis and refused to let any Ethiopian nationals board planes.

The cabinet was in emergency session all day, and finally announced that a four-man committee led by Foreign Minister Zewde Gebre Selassie, had been set up to negotiate with the armed forces. In the evening the military announced an 11 pm to 6 am curfew and set up a tight network of road blocks round the city. Just before curfew fell, truck-loads of troops were seen emerging from Fourth Division Headquarters. When I asked one of the young soliders guarding RVOG what was going on he said simply: 'We're tired of what is happening to our country. Now we're going to do something about it.'

Early on Sunday morning, June 30, Emperor Haile Selassie went to church as usual, disproving reports that he had been taken out of the city the previous evening.

At the home of Ras Asrate Kassa, members of his family were still trying to persuade him to flee to the countryside. But the proud nobleman refused to run away. He told a relative 'If they want me they can come for me. Meantime, I'm going to church.'

Shortly after he left, four jeeps loaded with heavily-armed soldiers arrived at the house. Leaving half the troops on guard at the house, the officer in charge, Colonel Ayalu, ordered one of the Ras's sons, Mulugeta, to accompany him and the rest of the soldiers to the church. They waited outside until the service was over, then sent Mulugeta in to fetch his father.

With all the innate dignity of his royal blood, Ras Asrate quietly walked to the waiting soldiers. A nervous Colonel Ayalu – who knew Ras Asrate personally – was fumblingly trying to light a cigarette. As he drew level, Ras Asrate pulled out a lighter. 'Allow me, Colonel,' he said. 'I take it you want me to come with you.'

Thus was the second most powerful man in the Ethiopian empire arrested. It was the AFC's most daring step to date.

73

There had been considerable speculation as to the whereabouts of the newly-arrested prisoners. The old cabinet was in an army base on the outskirts of Addis and some of the new prisoners had been taken there. That evening a contact phoned me to say he'd heard that an 'overflow' was being housed in the Imperial Golf Club pavilion. I was in the telex office with a colleague when the call came through and we decided that we'd make a slight detour past the golf course on our way home.

As we rounded a corner near the clubhouse we were confronted by a huge army truck parked across the road. Even as I braked, half a dozen shouting soldiers, rifles at the ready, raced towards us. They were extremely nervous and were all talking at once. I explained we were just going home, showed my I/D card, and they grudgingly allowed us to drive round the truck on the grass verge – and warned us to go slowly along the 'no-man's land' to another army truck blocking the road at the other side of the pavilion. 'We have orders to shoot anyone driving along the road between these trucks,' explained one of the soldiers. It wasn't the most reassuring thing he might have said as he waved us through. Fortunately a great deal of shouting between these soldiers and those a few hundred yards up the road prevented the second batch from carrying out their orders!

The soldiers had cause to be nervous. Inside the building, we found out later, was their 'number one' prisoner to date – Ras Asrate Kassa.

The arrests of members of the ruling class and senior officials continued throughout that night.

Enter the Dergue (July 2-3)

On Tuesday, July 2 the military started broadcasting in the name of the 'Armed Forces Co-ordinating Committee'. This was the first time the description had been used publicly by the military, and the first admission that the military movement had become institutionalized. It was the birth of the 'Dergue', the term by which the committee would become commonly known. Even Ethiopians disagree on the exact meaning of the word in English. Much of

Amharic is untranslatable with any degree of accuracy, since it is a language of concepts rather than words. In the context of the military movement, however, the nearest translation of 'Dergue' is simply a committee of equals. It was to become a very sophisticated body, but in those early days of July, it was still in embryo – and its use in communiqués disguised the fact that it by no means represented all opinion within the armed forces.

However, although there was general agreement that action was needed, a number of units – particularly the Imperial Bodyguard – while wanting to rid the country of corrupt officials were unwilling to be party to the arrests of such powerful people as Ras Asrate Kassa.

Faced with this delicate situation, the radicals in the Armed Forces Co-ordinating Committee knew they had to proceed with caution, without alarming the public – or the ordinary policeman and soldier. For no one knew what the reaction would be if it appeared that the Emperor himself was being threatened. Hence their repeated expressions of loyalty, and their assurances that the military only wanted to clear the decks, as it were, to allow the civilian administration to function properly and get on with reforms.

At that stage, most ordinary soldiers probably genuinely believed in this course. Certainly few would have supported a move against the Emperor. But the radical leaders of the Dergue had a definite aim in mind. Around the end of June and beginning of July, therefore, the foundations were secretly laid for the careful, step-by-step programme of propaganda and action to woo and unify public and military that was to reach its climax in September.

An Ethiopian friend once remarked to me that the difficulty of assessing events in his country was that in Ethiopia even the tip of the iceberg was hidden. Certainly the originators of that scheme have so far remained obscure, but there is reason to believe that among the key men whose ideas shaped the plan was a bright, foreign-trained young captain, Tefera Teklehaimanot, from the Third Division at Harar, although the 'honours' were later to be claimed by another Third Division soldier – Major Mengistu Haile Mariam. But behind them was one of the most brilliant military

75

strategists in the country, the former head of the Harar Military Academy, and one-time Commander of the Third Division, Major General Aman Andom.

Within twenty-four hours of that first public revelation that there was such a thing as an Armed Forces Co-ordinating Committee, Haile Selassie made his first statement since the beginning of the latest military activity. It was to announce that Lt.-General Wolde-Selassie Bereke had been removed from his top military post and given a seat in the Senate. In his place as Chief of Staff of the Armed Forces was Aman Andom.

Power Sharing (July 3-8)

Wednesday, July 3 was the day Emperor Haile Selassie joined the revolution.

In the morning the government delegates, led by the Foreign Minister, had again met the Armed Forces Committee. It seemed to Dejazmatch Zewde a stalemate situation. The government was impotent in the face of the military activity, yet the military kept pledging allegiance to the Emperor and saying they were only acting in support of the Endalkatchew government. Angrily the Minister turned on the soldiers: 'Look, it can't go on like this. What do you want? Either you let *us* run the country – or you take over.'

That afternoon, when faced with a similar challenge by Haile Selassie, the rebel soldiers refused to take full control. But they also refused to return to barracks and loose their hold on the country. Instead they presented the Emperor with a list of demands: the release of all political prisoners – except for those they themselves had arrested since February; amnesty for all political refugees; an extension of the current session of Parliament to speed up work on the new constitution and various urgent social measures; and close cooperation between the civilian government and the military.

Finally, in another meeting with the Committee, the Emperor agreed to the list of demands, and the problem of the last demand about cooperation was solved by giving the Armed Forces Co-ordinating Committee semi-permanent status as an official body for as long as it took the government to meet their demands.

Furthermore, the Emperor agreed to be identified with the military movement, and to allow it to be announced that the new government-military partnership had *his* blessing. But as the Committee members left the room, Haile Selassie was heard to remark to one of his aides that he wasn't going to be dictated to 'by a bunch of upstart young soldiers'.

On July 4 the armed forces announced the dissolution of the National Security Commission, which they had seen as an 'arm' of the establishment to suppress the reform movement. And for the first time, the military's communiqué was signed off with the phrase first used in that *Ethiopian Herald* editorial at the end of February: 'Ethiopia Tikdem' (Ethiopia First). This, said the Committee, was to be the motto of the movement.

On the morning of July 8, the Committee made its first detailed disclosures about the arrests so far, and announced a wanted list of twenty-seven aristocrats, military and defence chiefs, former ministers and government officials. They were given until that evening to surrender, or have their property confiscated. Anyone helping them to escape would have to 'answer to the armed forces'.

Key figure on the list was the powerful Ras Mesfin Shileshi – who at one time, it was said, could have commanded an army of 200,000 men. Now it was thought he could barely muster a few dozen, but his reputation as one of the heroes of the fight against the Italian occupation in the '30s presented the military with a few headaches.

Also on the list were the cream of the Crown Council and Senate, and top figures in government, police and provincial administration.

If the aims of the original Armed Forces Committee which organized the February Revolt had been thwarted because its enemies were still at large, this new Committee was making no such mistake. The gloves were off now, and anyone even remotely connected with repressive conservative elements, with the failure to combat the Wollo drought and famine, or with the faintest taint of corruption, was a candidate for detention.

77

The Thirteen-Point Charter (July 9-12)

To the observer, the situation at this time was still confused, as far as the relationship between the government and the military was concerned. That confusion was dispelled on Tuesday, July 9 when the Co-ordinating Committee issued its 'Thirteen-Point Charter'. It began by quoting the motto 'Ethiopia First' and pledging loyalty to their Commander-in-Chief, the Emperor. It went on to state that 'the fundamental objectives and aims of the Co-ordinating Committee' were 'to uphold the Crown of His Imperial Majesty ... and to ensure the smooth functioning of the new cabinet by removing any obstacles from within or outside the Cabinet'.

The rest of the document, however, made it clear – without putting it in so many words – that these expressions of loyalty and support were conditional upon the Committee's aims for the country being implemented. 'You're running the country,' it said in effect to the Emperor and cabinet, 'but we're running you'.

The document affirmed that 'close cooperation between the Council of Ministers and the Co-ordinating Committee is proper and essential to enable the Committee to present proposals and to ensure their implementation.' The document concluded: 'The Co-ordinating Committee believes that this military movement will achieve lasting changes without any bloodshed. The culture and history of Ethiopia are unique, so is the nature and course of this military movement.' It was the most comprehensive statement yet made by the armed forces.

Meanwhile, the Commission of Inquiry into Corruption was revitalized and increased from seven to fifteen. It included six representatives named by, but not members of, the Chamber of Deputies, and one each from, or nominated by, the ground forces, the air force, the navy, the Imperial Bodyguard, the Territorial Army, the police, the Ethiopian Teachers' Association, the University Lecturers' Association and the Auditor-General's Office – but not the Auditor General himself. He had been arrested! The Commission was to be chaired by Professor Mesfin Wolde-Mariam, an expert on land reform and a radical who had once been imprisoned by Haile Selassie for his criticism of the feudal regime.

There had been a flood of arrests and surrenders that week and on Friday, July 12 two of the men who, it was feared, might raise opposition to the Committee, gave themselves up. One was Dejazmatch Worku, the eldest member of the notorious Enqu-Selassie family – virtual rulers of large parts of Western Ethiopia. Many had thought he would join up with his two younger brothers who had let it be known they would not give up without a fight. The other was the man considered 'public enemy number one' – Ras Mesfin Shileshi.

In the meantime CELU – which only a couple of weeks previously had been almost at war with the military – issued a statement in support of the Armed Forces Co-ordinating Committee and praising the way the military had taken into account, in its 'Charter', the needs of the workers. It was an outward indication of the growing support for the armed forces.

On the Thursday of that week RVOG broadcast a commentary I had written for its daily 'Topic' programme on the current Ethiopian situation which reflected my own mood of optimism and admiration for the way the military had handled events – a mood I still believe was shared by most people in Ethiopia at the time, nationals and foreigners alike.

Referring to coups d'état in general, I wrote: 'Instead of sweeping away the good with the bad as so often happens in such situations, the Ethiopian Military Movement has tried to weave a careful path through the minefield of conflicting loyalties, centuries-old traditions, intrigue, entrenched conservatism and the growing awareness of the need for change and reform which characterizes Ethiopia today. The armed forces ... can be justifiably proud of their boast that what has been achieved has been done so far without bloodshed. But no amount of change in the ruling structures of the country will achieve anything unless there is a basic change of heart in the people – and in Ethiopia's case a people who have lost heart and lost the drive to help themselves under the weight of a system which took everything and gave very little.'

Murder at the Mosque (July 13–21)

The ELF had not remained inactive during this period.

On Saturday, July 13 Dejazmatch Hamid Feraeg Hamid, one of three Moslems with the rank of Minister of State on the five-men Provincial Council, went to the mosque as usual in his home town of Agordat, about a hundred miles west of Asmara. He was at prayers when a group of men burst into the building and shot him.

Dejazmatch Hamid, former President of the old Federal Assembly of Eritrea, had become the second victim of the 'death squad' of the ELF, which was determined to wipe out all collaborators with the Ethiopian regime.

It was obviously of some assistance to the guerillas that the Ethiopian army was preoccupied with other matters. By now the Second Division in Asmara was going through its own programme of arrests.

On July 17 eight armoured vehicles surrounded the palace of provincial governor, Lt.-General Debebe Haile Mariam. Shortly afterwards it was announced that he, his deputy and five other provincial officials had been arrested. Then at 6 pm the military announced on Radio Asmara that a curfew would start in two hours' time. Anyone seen on the streets would be shot. The precaution proved unnecessary, but it had been taken in view of reliable reports that the ELF were planning an attack on the city.

Events were progressing in Addis meanwhile. On July 14 the Committee issued their strongest communiqué to date. It demanded the cooperation of the public and announced that until they had freed Ethiopia from its past and totally rid the country of maladministration they would not return to their barracks.

Defence Minister General Abiye Abebe was among those still at large. Though, remarkably, his name had never appeared on any wanted list, he had, however, been warned privately to surrender by Sunday, July 21 and some reports suggested he had been working in collaboration with the Eritrean Governor-General, General Debebe, in an attempt to get outside assistance.

But on July 16 General Abiye quietly surrendered. Apart from being the Emperor's son-in-law, Abiye Abebe had proved in the

1960 coup attempt not only his loyalty to Haile Selassie, but his ability to organize counter-moves against the rebels. To have him safely in their hands without bloodshed was quite an achievement for the military and the chances of armed opposition were considerably diminished.

The same day, a couple of incidents made it clear that the armed forces could not sit back and rest on their laurels. A routine search of a bus coming into the city – road checks on all routes in and out of the city had remained in force (and were to remain well into 1975, with varying degrees of intensity) – uncovered forty-five weapons, including automatic rifles, hidden in bags on the luggage rack. And under a bridge near the British Embassy a sackful of small bombs and hand-grenades was found by a group of children.

The incidents increased tension in the city, and that evening extra troops appeared on the streets and heavily-armed guards were placed around the main petrol depots and at the transmitter sites of Radio Ethiopia and RVOG.

And all the while the propaganda increased in frequency and intensity, with lengthy statements on radio denouncing the rich in the Ethiopian establishment as bloodsuckers, and calling on the people to rise up and take their rightful place in Ethiopian society.

It was beginning to sound a bit more like a revolution.

Plot Within A Plot (July 22-26)

Lij Endalkatchew Makonnen, Prime Minister since February 28, was obviously now living on borrowed time as far as the Premiership was concerned. He was, after all, the only senior member of the Aklilu cabinet still not in detention, and the only mystery was how he had survived so long.

On July 22 he resigned – at the insistence of the Armed Forces Co-ordinating Committee. His replacement was Lij Michael Imru.

The Emperor's acquiescence averted a potential drama known only to a few extreme radical members of the Armed Forces co-ordinating Committee – which now numbered about eighty. The day after Endalkatchew's resignation was the Emperor's 82nd birthday, when at 6 am he would, according to his custom, go to church. Had Haile Selassie been reluctant to oust Endalkatchew, or had he refused to lend his name to the appointment of Michael Imru, the 'hard core' of the Dergue would have had him arrested on his way to church, with all his highborn retinue: his family would have been rounded up, and Ethiopia would have been taken over completely by the armed forces. A republic would have been declared, with General Aman installed as President. Whether or not General Aman was behind the plan, or even knew of it, and whether or not it would have succeeded, we shall probably never know. But the plot existed.

The manner of Endalkatchew's 'resignation' had immediately started speculation as to when he would be arrested. And the odds on it being sooner rather than later seemed to shorten considerably, when two days after the announcement, Radio Ethiopia launched a bitter attack on the ousted Premier, warning that the same measures would be taken against him as had been taken against the former ministers and officials, with whom he shared full responsibility for the failures of the Aklilu government. It also accused him of working to divide the armed forces, and went on to broaden the attack to the detainees, pointing out that the armed forces were 'not impressed by their crocodile tears considering such people ignored the real tears of the poor under centuries of oppression by the ruling classes'.

Michael Imru arrived back in Addis the following day, July 25, and was met at the airport – significantly – not by the Emperor, who had, according to all the statements, appointed him, but by the Army Chief of Staff, General Aman Andom.

Next day, July 26, the long-awaited Commission of Inquiry into Corruption actually began to look as if it would start when its chairman, Professor Mesfin, held a press conference to outline its aims, and describe how it would work.

Throughout the press conference, the Professor had at his side the Commission's vice-chairman, Major Mersha Admassu, who occasionally 'interpreted' the Professor's replies and added his own thoughts. Professor Mesfin, however, blandly stated that there was no connection between the military and the Commission – except that the armed forces had promised to support it. It wasn't a very convincing performance.

Afterwards, at the end of a private interview, he affected condescension: 'I'm told there is a revolution going on here. If there is, it's a legal revolution. The trouble with you Western journalists is that you don't understand how we do things here.' The Major – who had insisted on staying with us throughout the interview – didn't look too pleased when I suggested the trouble was that some of us had understood only too well what was going on!

'Hippy' Ambassador – Unhappy Premier (July 27 – August 1)
The month ended with the granting of amnesty to thirty-five people accused of political crimes; a statement from the ELF secretary-general, Osman Saleh Sabbi, calling for recognition of the ELF as the sole representative of Eritrea and demanding a referendum of independence under UN supervision; and the swearing-in of the new Prime Minister.

Like Haile Selassie, Lij Michael's father was a direct descendant of King Sahle Selassie, last of the great independent rulers of Shoa, hub of the Amhara-dominated Empire. But his father's socialist views had rubbed off on Lij Michael, and his outspoken attacks on conservative values over the years had made him an enfant terrible of the establishment. They also earned him 'banishment' as an ambassador to get him out of the way. And while serving – appropriately – in Moscow, his practical socialism would not allow him to use his diplomatic privileges and he would often be seen in shop queues with ordinary Muscovites. He was a particular champion of Ethiopian students in Russia, and squeezed an extra allowance for them out of the Addis government. He had refused to have his office redecorated when he went to Moscow because he thought the money could be put to better use. Ethiopia's man in Moscow had, in fact, become nicknamed the 'hippy ambassador'.

This image, however, didn't convince everyone and within a few days of his appointment as Premier, pamphlets began appearing denouncing him, criticizing the Armed Forces Committee, and, for the first time, openly attacking the Emperor. One, headed 'Government by aristocrats – for how long?' pointed out that Lij Michael was a relation of Endalkatchew, that his appointment had 'disappointed the peasant and the working class who have now realized that the promises made by the Co-ordinating Committee are false', and added 'the exploiting aristocratic class, led by Emperor Haile Selassie, has found it necessary to replace its discredited sons, kin and puppets by their likes to perpetuate itself. Within the Co-ordinating Committee itself there are pro-Haile Selassie elements who try to destroy the efforts of genuine and progressive members ... If the country's difficulties are to be overcome, the aristocratic regime must be destroyed completely.'

In fact, Prime Minister Lij Michael was already heading for failure even as he was being sworn in. He was convinced – and was to remain so until the last moment – that there was no serious threat to the Emperor, and that the armed forces would retain their supportive role. He was doubtless encouraged in this view by those conservative elements within the Committee who believed their own recent statement that 'the country should be run by civilians'.

However, on August 1 *The Ethiopian Herald* carried a joyful report from the Committee that letters were 'flowing en masse' into their headquarters from all over the country, carrying messages of support and exhorting the committee 'not to be slow in executing its decisions so that reactionary forces will not be able to organize and counter the committee's reform efforts and keep the revolutionary spirit of the people alive.'

The implications didn't seem to leave much room for an effective civilian Prime Minister.

The die was cast, and the true radicals on the Committee were already steering events the way they wanted them to go. Even as the Prime Minister was reading his morning paper that first day of August, the hard-line leaders in the Dergue were on their way to the Grand Palace to see the Emperor. The letter writers – if, indeed, they existed – need have had no fear that reactionaries would be given time to organize.

8 Junta in the Wings

The Net Tightens (August 1-6)

Inside the Palace the eighty-two year old Emperor was grim as he faced the Committee's representatives. They had yet another wanted list, headed by ex-Premier Endalkatchew, who was already under virtual house arrest. But Haile Selassie had had enough. He refused to sanction any further arrests, possibly still under the illusion that his word alone had the power to stop the Committee He was soon disabused of that idea.

When Haile Selassie said 'No' once again, the leader of the group of young officers turned to his men and, indicating the Emperor's personal bodyguard, Colonel Tassew Wajo, snapped: 'Take him!'

Within the next few hours Endalkatchew, the Commander of the Fourth Division, Major General Tadesse Melke, prominent Crown Councillor Abebe Retta — who'd been Agriculture Minister for a time in Aklilu's cabinet, former Air Force Commander Major General Abera Wolde-Mariam, and two high court judges were among nine people arrested.

For the leading radicals on the Dergue, the pretence of loyalty to the Emperor was over, though they would still use his name when it suited them. Haile Selassie, once absolute ruler of an Empire, was now reduced to sitting impotently by while his relatives and close advisers were arrested by a 'bunch of upstart young soldiers'.

Meantime Michael Imru had been working on his cabinet, and on August 3 — ignoring instructions to consult the Dergue first — he announced seventeen names, including that of General Aman Andom as Minister of Defence in addition to his existing post as Chief of Staff of the Armed Forces. For the first time in fifteen years Ethiopia also had a Deputy Prime Minister – Dejazmatch Zewde Gebre Selassie, who also retained his post as Foreign Minister. However, ten of the seventeen names were carried over from the Endalkatchew administration; four of them were distinctly displeasing to the Dergue, and indeed one of them was on the list for imminent arrest!

The Committee was furious. But at this crucial stage in their plot they could not afford to provoke another crisis.

Lij Michael refused point-blank to sack the offending Ministers. And if the military tried to arrest any members of his cabinet while they were still in office, he would resign.

A compromise was therefore reached. Michael Imru would allow the dust to settle on his new cabinet for a while, and then would announce a slight reshuffle – shuffling out the man they wanted, and shuffling to the sidelines those who had displeased the Committee.

At the same time, on the advice of the Anti-Corruption Commission, orders were given for the arrest of twenty-eight judges, including a member of the Emperor's private court, the 'Chilot', which on his orders could overrule the decision of any court in the land.

'A free, democratic Ethiopia' (August 7)

Under pressure from the impatient military the Commission set up to revise the 1955 Constitution and been working furiously to get their report ready within the six months deadline. On August 7 the Commission's chairman released a summary of the main points of what he called the 'draft' revision.

It proposed nothing less than the total abolition of the feudal system of government and the complete stripping of executive, legislative and judiciary powers from the Emperor, reducing him and any future monarch to a mere symbol. It spelt the end for a system that had held Ethiopia in bondage for centuries.

The Emperor would be a 'symbol of unity' and a constitutional monarch. He must be an Orthodox Christian. The succession would be decided by age and with no distinction as to sex. There would be no 'Chilot' and the monarch would not be allowed to make any appointment to any branch of government or the judiciary. The new constitution omitted article 31 of the 1955 version, which gave the Emperor the right to distribute property and land to those he favoured – a right enjoyed by Ethiopian monarchs for centuries and used very effectively by Haile Selassie to maintain his power.

In relation to the government and the law, it was proposed that the executive, legislative and judicial branches would work in conjunction – and not, as under Haile Selassie, as separate entities responsible only to him. Instead of a Crown Council, Senate and Prime Minister appointed by the Emperor and a lower House of Parliament powerless over the other branches of government, there would in future be two houses – a Lower Shengo (Assembly) and an Upper Shengo, which together would comprise the supreme governmental institution in the land, a National or People's Assembly. The National Assembly would choose the Prime Minister, who in turn would choose his cabinet – and all would be answerable to the National Assembly. Premiers would be elected for four years, and ministers would not be allowed to engage in any profitable business.

The Lower Shengo would be elected by the people. The Upper Shengo would be an assembly of ninety people, seventy-five elected by local government councils throughout the country, and fifteen nominated by the cabinet.

The Church and State were to be separate, and religion a matter of conscience. Civil rights and duties would be more clearly defined. Freedom of speech and of the press, and the right to form political and other associations and trade unions would be safeguarded, and political parties would be allowed 'irrespective of tribe, religion or race'. There would be a complete overhaul of education, health and employment legislation. Education would be free, work opportunities and facilities would be expanded, and a social security system developed. The voting age would be lowered to eighteen, and there would be stricter controls on eligibility to stand for public office. Government land would be made available for agricultural use and there would be a limit on land holdings. But private property was to be considered sacred, although the government could nationalize in the interests of the nation.

It was, for Ethiopia, a remarkably progressive document, and had in it the makings of what, in another RVOG 'Topic' programme, I called 'a free, democratic Ethiopia'.

However, though it *was* a brave and commendable attempt to drag Ethiopia into the twentieth century, the proposals left many important areas rather vague, and had written into them a proviso that much would be subject to subsequent clarification by legislation.

The relationship between the Emperor and the Church was still unclear, and the fact that Orthodox Christianity would remain the official religion of the country was not likely to please the Moslems.

Even more important in many eyes, the proposals only skimmed the surface of what most radicals regarded as the root cause of the country's problems – the need for land reform on a vast scale.

Establishment reaction to the new Constitution came in the form of a statement by the Patriarch of the Orthodox Church, Abune Tewoflos, who critized the armed forces and denounced many of the measures in the Revised Constitution.

One of the most outspoken of the radical critics was the head of the university's Political Science Department, Dr. Negussie Ayele, who was to be the architect of a later policy statement defining Ethiopian socialism. In particular he was concerned about the qualifying phrase 'in accordance with future laws', which had been in the 1955 Constitution and had been used by the Emperor to sidestep any part of the Constitution which worked against his personal interests or those of his establishment.

And within the Dergua one cause of considerable dissatisfaction among the hard-liners was the provision allowing for the creation of political parties. But the Dergue was busy with more immediate problems.

Show of Strength (August 8-15)

Behind the new wave of arrests of the Emperor's inner circle of advisers was a two-fold purpose. On the one hand, it was an integral part of the plan to isolate the Emperor, but the more immediate reason was the discovery of yet another Palace plot against the Dergue. Approaches had been made to officers thought to be loyal to the establishment – particularly within the Imperial Bodyguard – with offers of land in return for support should any move be made against the Emperor. The plot had been reported to the Dergue, who were now picking off those involved.

Key men in this plot were General Assefa Demissie, the Emperor's Chief ADC, Blatta (an honorary title) Admassu Retta, Haile Selassie's personal treasurer, and Solomon Gebre-Mariam, the Emperor's private secretary – whose arrest had been ordered on August 5. Between them they had prepared 'certificates' giving title to land and were ready to distribute them when the Dergue moved. On August 10 the Committee announced that General Assefa had had to be detained 'forcefulhy, thereby disgracing himself', and gave the other two until that afternoon to surrender. A list of other newly-arrested officials – mainly from the provinces – was issued at the same time.

Two days later the *Herald* carried a fierce attack on ex-Premier Endalkatchew and his Defence Minister, General Abiye, accusing them of creating the now-disbanded National Security Commission as a 'repressive organization against the labour movement' and alleging that the Commission had used 'the most inhuman methods of torture and manhandling' of labour leaders and telecommunications and power workers. It had also broken up a strike at a farm in Sidamo province by 'simply shovelling two thousand workers into trucks by force and putting them into a camp'. The chairman of the NSC, ex-army Chief of Staff Lt.-General Wolde Selassie Bereke, was alleged to have told the leaders of the telecommunications strike that if they did not obey the Commission's orders, 'We will kill you, we will beat you, we will hang you, we will flog you.' It was good rousing stuff, calculated to get the people into the right mood for what was to come.

On Thursday, August 15 the Dergqa announced the dissolution of the Ministry of Pen – the ancient inner group of officials most closely connected with the Emperor, responsible for his most confidential affairs, and used by him to dispense favours and gifts.

Next morning there was briefly near-panic when, unannounced, squadrons of American-built F.5 fighter-bombers buzzed the city, zooming at roof level over the Palace. Then into the streets of the city centre poured an impressive parade of tanks, armoured vehicles, recoil-less anti-tank field guns and scores of jeeps and lorry-loads of soldiers, air force men and policemen. After the initial shock, the public turned out to give them the most demonstrative reception seen in the streets of the capital since Haile Selassie's return from exile at the end of the Italian occupation.

Car and window stickers bearing the motto 'Ethiopia First' were handed out by the troops, and the military vehicles were plastered with the 'Ethiopia First' symbol superimposed on a map of Ethiopia. Street hawkers were suddenly selling 'Ethiopia Tikdem' T-shirts.

The demonstration was by no means just a publicity stunt. It was a massive display of military solidarity for the benefit of elements in the Imperial Bodyguard, led by its Commander, Lt.-General Tafesse Lemma, who were still opposing the movement and had again threatened to use force to release some of the detainees. This intimidating physical warning was backed up by a communiqué which stated bluntly that the armed forces were 'prepared to shoot and destroy' anyone who got in their way.

The show of strength also coincided with an announcement that the Emperor's private court had been abolished, as had the Crown Council – ten of whose forty members were already in detention. The Emperor's Chief of Staff of the Palace Guard – the only important member of his inner circle still not detained – had been transferred, it was disclosed, to another post within the Ministry of Defence.

The heaviest blow to the Emperor's authority had undoubtedly been the abolition of his cherished Crown Council, the main channel of his power. The dissolution of the Chilot had taken away his feudal role as supreme law-giver, and the removal of his personal bodyguard and personal military staff – through which the Palace had become, over the years, almost a state within a state – had left Haile Selassie an empty shell.

Next day the Dergue announced the arrest of the Commander of the Bodyguard, General Tafesse. The last source of effective opposition within the armed services had been neutralized.

So far the direct attacks had been on the trappings surrounding the Emperor. Now the campaign against the monarchy itself started. On August 16 the Amharic paper *Addis Zemen* carried a lengthy summary of opinion on the recently-announced draft constitution, which included the following statement by the Public Relations Officer of the Ethiopian Grain Board – a government employee – Haile Mariam Goshu: 'The draft constitution is not a solution, nor does it attack the real causes of the present social, political and economic problems ... the monarchy has discredited the Ethiopian people by taking away their identity and reputation and in short is the cause for the retarded material state of the country.'

In the middle of the previous week one of my contacts had come up with a fascinating list of hearsay and predictions. The Dergue had got hold of the Emperor's private files when they closed down the Ministry of Pen and were about to make use of the information in them. The military were dissatisfied with Michael Imru and he would last at the most three months as Premier. They were also concerned about the recovery of the Emperor's fortune abroad, particularly his gold, and would be making propaganda capital out of this. Haile Selassie would be 'out' within two months; Aman Andom would emerge as the new Head of State. The first thing the new military rulers would do when they ousted the Emperor would be to dissolve Parliament and suspend the Constitution.

My contact also predicted that Professor Mesfin Wolde Mariam would not survive as chairman of the Anti-Corruption Commission, and that the one man who would survive the period unscathed and still in office would be Foreign Minister Zewde Gebre Selassie.

His predictions were uncannily accurate. He was also to give me three days' warning of the outbreak of hostilities in Eritrea the following February. But in mid-August, Eritrea came into the news for a different – though not unconnected – reason.

Olive Branch to Eritrea (August 16-19)

The preoccupation of the Committee with the problems of controlling the centre had not passed unnoticed by the Eritrean guerillas, whose raids became more daring. It had also angered the province's twenty-three MPs in the Chamber of Deputies. On August 16 they sent a long statement to Parliament outlining the Eritrean case, and pointing out that in July – while the then Prime Minister Endalkatchew was supposedly working on a solution that he had promised after seeing a delegation of Eritrean MPs – women and children and aged were being massacred by government troops in a raid in Om-Hajer District. Since the present administration had shown similar indifference to the Eritrean situation, the MPs had decided to quit.

Four days later, during a debate in the Chamber on the resignation of the twenty-three MPs, both Lij Michael and General Aman Andom were given permission to address the House on the issue. The Premier stated that 'all Ethiopians have been following with sadness and anxiety the lack of peace and security and in some cases the shedding of blood among brothers in some districts of Eritrea in recent years'. But while the new government would not give in to 'force and blackmail', it would, he said, 'spare no effort' to solve the Eritrean problem and would seek a 'political solution in consultation with the genuine leaders of the people'.

He did not say who these leaders might be, but it was remarkable that such comments had been made at all by an Ethiopian Premier.

General Aman then took the floor and announced that the following Monday he would leave to tour Eritrea to make a first-hand assessment of the problems. Significantly, Aman was an Eritrean.

For the first time an Ethiopian government had openly acknowledged the Eritrean problem, and there were hopes that peace might be achieved. These hopes were somewhat dampened, however, when on August 25 an ELF communiqué from Cairo said the guerillas were 'agreeable in principle' to negotiation with the Ethiopian government to work out a political solution – but only if such agreement guaranteed full national independence, and if the Addis government recognized the ELF as the sole representatives of the Eritrean people. It called for a referendum supervised by the UN, the OAU and the Arab League.

General Aman's tour of Eritrea, however, turned out to be an unqualified personal success. He won over the Second Division immediately on arrival by insisting that he stay in their barracks and not in the governor's palace, and throughout the tour he maintained this habit of staying with the men. He addressed mass meetings of between 14,000 and 18,000 citizens and got rousing cheers when he blamed previous administrations for using 'religious and ethnic differences to divide Ethiopians and make them fight each other'.

Cynical observers, however, were not slow to point out that as well as taking some of the heat out of the Eritrean situation, General Aman was not neglecting his own popularity stakes.

'This is not a coup' (August 20-27)

In Addis, meantime, the anti-monarchist radicals on the Dergue were intensifying their propaganda campaign – which was aimed as much at those moderatas in their own ranks who wanted to retain the monarchy (and even Haile Selassie), as at the public.

On August 22 the weekly magazine *Ethiopia* carried the public attack straight to the Emperor – accusing him of 'squandering the nation's money on lavish journeys abroad'. The writer – an employee of the government news agency – aded that the monarchy was against the interests of the people. It concluded somewhat vividly by accusing the Emperor of 'defecating' on the people of Ethiopia. An Orthodox priest publicly questioned the Emperor's claim to descent from Solomon and Sheba, while other articles and letters accused him of being 'an expensive and unnecessary luxury'.

Then, on August 25, came the dramatic announcement that the Emperor's personal residence, the Jubilee Palace, had been

93

nationalized. In future it would be called the National Palace, and would be administered by a government-appointed manager.

Earlier that day rumours of trouble in the cabinet were confirmed when the Prime Minister announced a reshuffle which removed the Minister of Mines, Dejazmatch Tesfa Yohannes Berhe. Two hours later he was arrested. The military had once again got their way.

Next day, August 26, the military announced that the National Resources Commission – an organization established at the end of World War II to manage Italian estates, property and business – had been transferred into the control of the Ministry of Finance. The NRC had spread its influence over the years and now controlled property taken from political and other prisoners – and the whole business was under the control of the Emperor, who used its holdings to finance some of his gifts and favours. The significance of the transfer was that it effectively deprived Haile Selassie of much of his movable assets.

At the same time the military disclosed a list of people who had been granted huge tax exemptions by the Emperor. One man, for example, who owed E$90,000 (£18,000) a year in tax had consistently paid only E$3,000 (£600).

Haile Selassie was now utterly powerless, but he continued to function in the only way he knew, officiating on August 27 at the swearing-in of the new members of Michael Imru's reshuffled cabinet. It was noticed that most members of the Royal family and the few friends still free were living with him in the palace.

A lighter episode occurred when a document appeared, addressed to the Armed Forces Co-ordinating Committee and issued by 'Concerned Citizens', attacking the moral decay of the old regime, many of whose members, it said, had kept concubines – who also happened to be other men's wives. Ministers and officials had gained access to the wives by promoting their husbands, or handing out public funds, villas and cars. The document named twenty-one women involved – including the wife of a senior government department official who had been given title to the land on which the Princess Zauditu Hospital stood, plus money and a limousine in return for favours to someone 'connected with the Palace'.

The document had followed an official statement condemning the fact that the capital had no fewer than 350,000 prostitutes operating in 10,000 brothels!

On a more serious note, representatives of the Armed Forces Committee called together the members of the Ethiopian Journalists Association on August 27. The gathering was addressed by a major who had graduated in journalism from an American university – and appeared to know what he was talking about. He appealed to the journalists to support the movement and explained that 'the present military movement in Ethiopia is not a coup d'état. It is a revolution of the people staged by the armed forces of Ethiopia, not because we are the only conscious group in the country, but because we happen to have the power to do it. But unlike military takeovers elsewhere, the Ethiopian Armed Forces are not interested in taking power, but in freeing the country from the corruption and oppression of its centuries-old system.'

Later that day the Anti-Corruption Commission issued a report charging the entire government of ex-Premier Aklilu Habte Wold with what amounted to genocide for their handling of the Wollo drought. Three former ministers were singled out and charged with lying to the Ethiopian people. Former Interior Minister Legesse Bezu had lied in broadcasting that the people of Wollo had enough – even a surplus – of food, and that when the government had taken food to the area they could find no one in need of it. The former ambassador to Britain, Zewde Mekuria, was charged with denying facts reported by the BBC. And Mulatu Debebe, former Minister of Community Development, was condemned for repudiating as exaggeration a BBC report that 100,000 people were dying.

A few days later, another BBC report was to be the cause of official embarrassment.

The Emperor and I (August 26-29)
Actually, the overthrow of Emperor Haile Selassie was all my fault; it happened like this…

I had been given information I believed to be reliable that Haile

Selassie's movements had been restricted. He was still allowed to travel between his Palaces and to a nearby church, but that was all. Certain areas of the newly-renamed National Palace had also been placed 'off-limits' to him, and he was virtually confined to one wing of the building. He was unable to travel anywhere without a close bodyguard of hand-picked men. (In fact these were men totally loyal to the Dergue, dressed in the uniforms of the Imperial Bodyguard!) I had sat on the information for some days, feeling it was a bit hot to handle – one never knew which way events would go, and Ethiopian security had a pretty mean reputation.

Late on the evening of August 26, however, the story was confirmed by another reliable source, and in view of the attacks on the Emperor in the press, I decided it was now time to file the story to the BBC. I rounded it off by recording that informed sources now said there was a real possibility that Haile Selassie 'will either abdicate – which is not really in his character – or be deposed'.

The following day, August 27, one of the government officials responsible for resident correspondents like myself summoned me to his office, where he played over a tape recording of the BBC World Service news carrying the story about the Emperor as its first headline.

'That was your report, wasn't it?' he said. I nodded.

'The Prime Minister is very angry about it. In fact the whole cabinet is angry. They're in a meeting now to discuss what to do about it. I don't know what the outcome will be – but I have been told to give you a final warning.'

I pointed out that as I hadn't been given any previous warnings, this must surely be a first warning.

'First – and final,' said the official, a man I had come to know and like. Then, softening, he added, 'I'm truly sōrry about this, Mr. Thomson, but I have my orders. Michael Imru is furious with you. He believes that your report could tip the balance against the Emperor and put ideas into the heads of the military.'

I hadn't thought I had that much influence on Ethiopian affairs!

'The trouble is,' he went on, 'no one knows what is going on – least of all the cabinet. And I'm in the middle. I sometimes wish the

Dergue would lock me up – at least I would know where I was then.' (He was, in fact, to be removed from his post shortly after the military took over and was later reported dead in mysterious circumstances.)

At that point a major from the Dergue arrived. He asked the official what he had told me, and was informed that the Prime Minister wanted to make an example of me.

The major became very angry. 'He will do no such thing. A brief warning – that's all.'

The official broke into Amharic and there was an angry exchange, the gist of which (my Amharic was sketchy to say the least) was that the major didn't care what the Prime Minister said, the official would do what the Dergue told him, and so would the Prime Minister if it came to that!

I thought I had been forgotten until the major turned to me and said confidentially, 'You see, Mr. Thomson, the Committee discussed your BBC report this morning and I won't pretend they were happy. It's all a matter of timing. If what you suggested might happen was going to take place in, say, the next forty-eight hours, then it wouldn't matter. But we're not ready yet – and what we're afraid of is that if the Emperor feels he's about to be arrested, or is losing too much prestige in the eyes of the world, he just might commit suicide. It's not likely – but its a possibility. So we don't want you to speculate. Just check with me in future before filing news about the Emperor. The only people who know what is going to happen is the Co-ordinating Committee – and we're not telling anyone!' Then, almost as an afterthought, he added: 'I know you won't report any of this conversation. And don't worry about the Prime Minister. We've agreed you should have a warning. That's all there is to it.'

While this conversation was going on, Radio Ethiopia was broadcasting the following statement: 'A spokesman for the Ministry of Information said the BBC Correspondent in Addis Ababa had been given a last warning because of unfounded information on the present Ethiopian situation that could affect Ethiopian unity and progress.'

The following evening, Wednesday, August 28, I was having dinner in a quiet corner of a city restaurant with one of my contacts and a senior government official – who was, in fact, taking a bit of a risk being seen with me in the circumstances. We had barely started the soup when the manager called me to the phone. It was my wife, slightly agitated, with news that Ethiopian Secret Service agents had called for me. I was to report immediately to their offices in Duke of Harar Street. After talking it over with my dinner partners I decided to ignore the summons – not least because that particular branch of the Ethiopian security service had been dissolved a few weeks previously by the Dergue, and its chief officers arrested.

The following morning, Thursday, I was wakened by a telephone call just after six and ordered by a man claiming to be the colonel in charge of this service to be in his office by 7 am – or they would come for me. After informing the British Embassy I decided to go, leaving a colleague to try and contact one of my acquaintances in the Dergue.

For the rest of that day, in a dingy upstairs room with bare walls, bare floorboards and a bare, single bulb hanging from the ceiling, and seated between two burly security men, I was questioned and re-questioned about the story I had filed.

They refused at first to give any reason why or on whose authority I had been summoned. They were not charging me with any crime; they simply wanted to know where I had got the information that I'd used in the story for the BBC. Who were my contacts? Who did I know in the Dergue? By mid-afternoon they had got nowhere – and I had twice persuaded them to release me to contact an Embassy official. (I had made a prior arrangement to do this at set intervals to ensure that if I was slipped out of a back door and spirited away my captors wouldn't have too long a head start.)

Finally, after making me sign a statement which said I would tell them nothing and in which I added a protest 'that such questioning is still found necessary in a country where protestations are now being made in government statements and by the Armed Forces Committee that freedom of the press and speech is one of the aims and guarantees of the present movement', I was allowed to go.

But before they released me, they had calle in an Ethiopian journalist with whom I worked occasionally and whom they were also questioning in connection with the BBC story. While I had been out of the room he had overheard the colonel tell one of the other men that he was 'fed up with this', and that in any case they were 'only going through the motions' of an investigation 'to keep the Prime Minister happy'.

It was all I needed to know. As soon as I was released I telephoned the major who had assured me that the public warning would be the end of the business. He said he knew nothing about my interrogation and asked who had questioned me. 'The security branch in Duke of Harar Street,' I said.

'But that doesn't exist any more,' was his puzzled reply.

'I can assure you it does,' I said, 'and if your Committee isn't running it, perhaps you'd better find out who is. All they wanted to know was what I knew about what the Dergue was up to.'

In fact, Michael Imru's office had ordered the investigation, and it had been through his office that the Emperor had re-instated the civilian security branch. The truth was that right up until the last moment. Michael Imru refused to believe that the military were really planning to remove the Emperor. Even in the last few days of Haile Selassie's reign, he was still trying to insist that the Dergue's decrees should first go to the Emperor for signature!

Subsequent events were to prove, even to him, that the Dergue didn't need a BBC correspondent to give them any ideas as far as the Emperor was concerned.

Lulu And The Lion (August 28 – September 11)

The Dergue meantime had had rather more pressing business in hand than worrying about resident correspondents.

On the 28th they announced the nationalization of the country's biggest bus company — Anbassa — the Addis-based firm in which the Emperor and his family were the biggest shaeholders. The Committee's statement for the first time specifically named Haile Selassie and members of his family, listing their holdings.

For the next few days there was a spate of attacks on the Emperor – and the media were used to the full. A former political prisoner appeared on television and demanded that the Emperor be court-martialled, accusing him of selling out the country by fleeing at the time of the Italian invasion. (A view which had been shared at the time by a number of prominent Ethiopians who, nevertheless, remained loyal to him.) A Committee statement issued on August 31 stated categorically that Haile Selassie had deceived the people throughout his reign.

The communiqué referred to the Emperor as 'Negus' – meaning king, and in this context, used derogatively – instead of 'Negus Negiste', King of Kings. It also announced the names of friends of the Emperor whose children were being educated abroad at public expense. And it added: 'The history of Ethiopia during the reign of "King" Haile Selassie has been a very sad one. Those who have opposed his unjust rule' (here it named some student leaders) 'have been killed by government troops'. Haile Selassie had been 'the leader of the exploiters'.

As the statement was being transmitted, extra troops turned up at the radio and TV stations, and throughout the city massive security precautions were taken around public buildings. But if the military had feared adverse reaction to their attack on the Emperor, they were to be pleasantly surprised. People who a few months ago were prostrating themselves in the mud every time the Emperor's car passed by, were now calmly accepting his public denigration.

The attacks continued into September in the press and on the radio, where they were introduced with military music and the singing of the rousing revolutionary song 'Ethiopia Tikdem'. TV plays mocked the rich and titled Ethiopian establishment and attacked the whole basis of Ethiopian society as maintained by Haile Selassie. Indeed, the main weapon in the final stages of Ethiopia's revolutionary process was not the gun, but the cathode tube.

On September 5 there was a lengthy and involved TV statement about St. George's Brewery in Addis Ababa. The brewery had been established fifty years previously by a foreigner, had been taken over by the Italian occupation forces, and later by the Ethiopian government, who, after some persuasion, paid the original owner E$500,000 (£10,000) compensation, Later still, the Emperor appropriated it, using all the profits for himself, his family and his friends. In 1964, however, Haile Selassie donated all future proceeds to his two charitable organizations, the Haile Selassie Prize Trust, and the Haile Selassie I Foundation, and later made a will assigning the brewery to them on his death. Then, in 1973, the Emperor 'sold' the brewery and the land to the nation. It hadn't of course, been his to sell, but it cost public funds another E$1,660,000 (£350,000). Even after paying twice for the property, the state got nothing out of it, for the Emperor refused to give up the deeds, and continued to take the profits!

As proof, the TV screen showed a close-up of a cheque made out to the Emperor's private exchequer for E$94,000 (£18,800) dated as recently as July 1974. All told, said the statement, Haile Selassie had personally taken more than E$11,000,000 (£2,200,000) out of the organization over the years.

The upshot of all this was the announcement that the brewery had been nationalized and the Haile Selassie Prize Trust wound up and its name abolished.

The Dergue had continued rounding up reactionaries and on September 3 had pinned down the Enqu-Selassie brothers in the countryside near Ambo to the west of Addis. The men had refused to surrender, and in the ensuing gunfight, Dejazmatch Tsehayu Enqu-Selassie was killed. His brother, Fitawrari Tadesse, and a group of their supporters were captured.

The same day students had marched through Addis demonstrating against the Emperor. Remarkably, the report of the demonstration on Radio Ethiopia at 2 pm in Amharic had quoted the slogans the students were chanting – 'Kill the Emperor', 'Hang the Emperor' and 'Down with the Emperor'.

The drought, however, was the emotional factor on which much of the anti-imperial propaganda was based, and in the last few days posters had appeared in the streets – based on an idea first used by the ELF – which showed pictures of Wollo drought victims alongside pictures of the Emperor in his fine clothes, feeding large chunks of meat to his dogs. One dog in particular was a feature of the campaign: Haile Selassie's pet chihuaha, Lulu, which had died after a long and comfortable life on the royal lap. It had been buried in the Palace grounds with a fine headstone to mark the spot.

In their most bitter and scathing attack on the Emperor, on September 11, the Ethiopian New Year's day, the military put on a TV item devoted to the care lavished on the Emperor's dogs. In particular, the Committee accused the Emperor of 'building statues to dead dogs and feeding his live ones while hundreds of thousands were starving. Yet all the while he was calling the poor and hungry 'my beloved people!' A few days later they repeated the attack, and showed pictures of the headstone and the inscription which read: 'To Lulu – Our Beloved Dog. He has been with us in Europe, Latin America and Asia'. As my cynical Ethiopian friend commented: 'That's one dog's life most Ethiopians would have been glad of.'

The evening's TV programmes also included a specially 'doctored' version of Jonathan Dimbleby's film of the Wollo drought – intercut with shots of lavish society weddings, the Emperor drinking champagne, and cakes being flown in from Europe for his banquets. The point had been well and truly made.

New Year's Day had started with a traditional broadcast by the Patriarch, Abune Tewoflos. Only it wasn't so traditional. It should have begun and ended with a eulogy to the Emperor and the royal family. It didn't mention them at all; instead it finished with a prayer – for the Armed Forces Co-ordinating Committee.

The day ended even more dramatically. Troops swooped on the city house of the one member of the royal family they'd so far left untouched – the Emperor's eldest surviving daughter, Princess Tenagne-Work, a powerful woman widely believed to have been a strong influence on her father in his later years. As the news spread through the city, hundreds of people gathered round her palace and began chanting abuse against the royal family.

I had no sooner phoned the story into the BBC than an hour's notice was given that a curfew would start at 8 pm. A few minutes later all telephone and telex communication between Ethiopia and the outside world was cut off and the airport closed.

9 Birth of a Nation – End of an Empire

'God deposed!' (September 12)

As dawn stole over the sleeping capital on the morning of September 12, tanks and jeeps with mounted machine-guns took up positions around the National Palace, the Grand Palace, Parliament, the Municipality and in some of the city centre's main squares. And at 7 am Radio Ethiopia opened with a fanfare of martial music and the announcement that Haile Selassie had been deposed.

It had not only been a bloodless coup, but even a dignified one. A small group of officers went to the National Palace just after 6 am and after establishing themselves in the ornate library, summoned the Emperor. Haile Selassie, frail, but retaining the dignity that had made his titles 'King of Kings, Elect of God, Conquering Lion of the Tribe of Judah' sit less incongruously than they might have done on such a tiny figure, entered a few moments later.

He stood as proud and erect as his eighty-two years would allow while the officers formally read their proclamation. He was accused of corruption and neglect; told that he had abused the power and dignity of his office for fifty years for personal gain and to benefit his family and retainers. Only his eyes glistened as he was told he was too weak, mentally and physically, to shoulder the responsibility of office any longer. The declaration ended by informing the Emperor that he was now deposed, and replaced by a provisional military government.

Haile Selassie broke the awkward silence which followed: 'We have served our people in war and peace. If we have to step down for the good of our people, we will not oppose this.'

With obvious embarrassment, one of the young officers – addressing Haile Selassie as 'Your Majesty' – asked the Emperor to come with them.

'Where?' he asked sharply.

'To a place of safety. You'll see,' was the reply.

When the Emperor still made no move, three Ethiopian journalists who had been present at the invitation of the military to record the events for posterity, were asked to leave.

Ten minutes later, Haile Selassie, flanked by the officers and supported by his cousin, Ras Imru, was led out of the library to the side door of the Palace. At the foot of the short flight of steps was a small blue Volkswagen. The man who had for years been chauffeur-driven in huge Mercedes limousines stopped.

'What! In there?' he said to the officer holding the passenger seat forward to let him in the back. The officer nodded, and with a little persuasive assistance from Ras Imru, Haile Selassie climbed in and slumped in the back seat. In the driving seat was a captain, in battle-dress uniform. There was no ceremonial guard of outriders, only a jeep in front and behind.

As the small convoy swung out of the Palace gates, past a tank and more jeeps guarding the entrance, and into Menelik Avenue, the Emperor was seen to turn, as if to have a last view of the Palace. His view was obscured by a crowd of chanting, jeering young people who had somehow discovered what was going on.

Within the hour, a radio broadcast told Ethiopians that they were no longer under the 'oppressive rule' of Emperor Haile Selassie. The statement was dascribed as 'Proclamation 1 on the Establishment of a Provisional Military Government in Ethiopia', and headed 'Ethiopia Tikdem'.

It summarized what had been read to the Emperor; abolished Parliament – 'which has so far served not the nation but the ruling aristocratic class', suspended the constitution – which was 'designed to give absolute power to the Emperor while providing a democratic façade for the benefit of world public opinion ... and abrogates the natural rights of man'; and laid down the basis of a transitional military government.

The statement went on to list the first proclamations of this new government. It named Crown Prince Asfa Wossen as king-designate, to be crowned as soon as he returned to the country – but as a head of state 'with no power in the country's administrative and political affairs'.

The new Draft Constitution would be put into effect as soon as 'necessary improvements are made to include provisions reflecting the social, economic and political philosophy of the New Ethiopia and to safeguard the civil rights of the people'. Meanwhile, the Co-ordinating Committee of the Armed Forces would hold power and run the country until legal representatives could be elected. Until then, courts would continue to function and all existing laws be valid, all strikes and demonstrations were 'contrary to the motto "Ethiopia First"', and were banned, and special military courts were to be set up to deal with anyone disobeying these and any future orders, and to try all the detained officials. No appeals would be allowed after the decisions of the military court.

A later broadcast confirmed the closure of the airport and imposed a 7.30 pm-5 am curfew.

The coup had finally come – but as something of an anti-climax. Only the martial music and frequent use of the 'Ethiopia Tikdem' song on the radio and the tanks dotted round the city suggested anything out of the ordinary. By mid-morning, the shops were open, the streets busy with the normal daily activities of the city and the tanks festooned with garlands of flowers, donated by wellwishers – who were pulling them out of the public flowerbeds!

The soldiers had looked very tense at first. After all, it had so often been forecast that if any move was made against the Emperor, the masses would rise up to defend him. And in fact no one could be really sure until it happened that they wouldn't. But finding no antagonism, the soldiers, with their vehicles, helmets and tunics plastered with 'Ethiopia Tikdem' stickers, soon relaxed.

The apparent calm with which the removal of the Emperor was

received was due to a large extent to traditional Ethiopian conservatism. They are not a demonstrative race by nature, they do not welcoie change, and this, the greatest change of all, was treated with suspicion. The fact that it provoked no stronger emotion is a tribute to the carefully-orchestrated propaganda campaign of the armed forces. As one Ethiopian put it that day: 'The military have been tuning Ethiopia like a master handling a Stradivarius – now we'll see if they can play it as well.'

The more intelligent Ethiopians certainly had no illusions that Crown Prince Asfa Wossen would ever return – or was ever intended to. And the big question in everyone's mind was just how provisional the new military government intended to be.

For one small group of people, however, the removal of Haile Selassie seemed like the end of the world. These were the adherents of a sect known as the Ras Tafarians (so-called after Haile Selassie's pre-coronation name, Ras Tafari), who were mainly West Indian – particularly Jamaican – descendants of Ethiopian slaves. They believed that Haile Selassie was a god and had built up a religious cult around him. Ironically, in the land of their god there had never been more than forty Ras Tafarians, and by 1974 their numbers had dwindled to about twenty-five adults, with some children, living an uneasy and harsh life in the south-west of the country. They had made a pilgrimage from Jamaica in 1969 expecting to be allowed to live and worship at the feet – or at least not far from the Palace – of their god. Instead, extremely embarrassed, Haile Selassie had grudgingly given them some unfarmable land near Shashamane some 250 miles south of Addis and left them to their fate.

Now their god had been deposed. When contacted a few days later, they said they were saddened, but were still clinging to their faith. 'The spirit of our god still lives and will live eternally no matter what is done to the person of the Emperor.'

Later that day Radio Ethiopia announced that Prime Minister Michael Imru had been transferred to the post of Information Minister. Foreign Minister Zewde Gebre Selassie retained that post, but was no longer Deputy Prime Minister. And the man who had emerged as an all-in-one head of state and Premier – with a bewildering array of titles — was General Aman Andom. He retained his positions as Defence Minister and Chief of Staff of the Armed Forces, but in addition was Chief Minister, Convenor of the Council of Ministers, and Chairman of the Armed Forces Co-ordinating Committee. The last title was the most puzzling — since the General wasn't even a member of the Committee.

But RVOG's 'Topic' programme that evening, 'Ethiopia — End of an Empire, Birth of a Nation' summed up what most people felt: that it was the dawning of a new ara.

New Regime – Old Problems (September 13-25)

The first sign that everything might not be quite what it seemed came the following day when there was a series of contradictory statements on the role of General Aman. The main question centred on whether or not he was chairman of the Dergue. Finally that day it was officially announced that General Aman *was* chairman.

Attention was cleverly diverted from what was going on inside the new corridors of power, however, with a renewal of the campaign of public denigration of the Emperor, and the 18,000-strong Ethiopian Teachers' Association ended their week of General Assembly meetings with a resolution asking the Committae to court-martial the Emperor 'for robbing the Ethiopian people and refusing to hand back to the state his illegally-amassed fortune'.

The Emperor's fortune — most of it allegedly in Swiss banks — was now the main target of the campaign. And the chief topic of conversation was the fate — and whereabouts — of the Emperor and his family. Rival news agencies put out stories, stating categorically that he was being held in locations eighty miles apart!In fact it appears he was moved around for several days to various places in Addis before being brought back to Fourth Division HQ and housed in the Commander's quarters.

The first open opposition to the new regime came from the same source which had opposed the Emperor — the students. On Monday, September 16 they went ahead with a demonstration in defiance of the ban on such gatherings, and paraded through the streets of the capital demanding immediate civilian rule. The military turned out in strength, especially around the university, but no attempt was made to disperse the thousands of students.

Later that afternoon officers from the Dergue went to Arat Kilo and mingled with the students, explaining that they genuinely had no intention of holding onto power longer than was necessary.

The Provisional Military Administrative Council (PMAC) – as the former Armed Forces Co-ordinating Committee now claimed to be – meanwhile issued a further 'clarification' of General Aman's role. He was *not* the chairman of the Dergue. He was its 'spokesman'. The Committee, which by now numbered 120 members, would, collectively, be the head of state, although General Aman would sign state papers, meet visiting dignitaries and accept ambassadors' credentials. The statement added that a body of civilians would be chosen by the PMAC to act as advisers to the military government.

But the students had a strong ally in their demand for civilian rule – the labour organization, CELU. After hearing the PMAC's statement, its leaders issued a six-page resolution stating that they firmly opposed 'the establishing of Provisional Military Rule' and that the PMAC's first proclamation had 'denied the basic human rights of assembly, of strike, peaceful demonstration and others'.

The CELU statement added that its members opposed the crown and demanded its complete abolition, and were strongly against the substitution of the Crown Prince for Haile Selassie.

It also criticized the announcement – made a few days before the Emperor was deposed – that students and teachers were to be prepared to take part in a National Work Campaign aimed at eradicating illiteracy and teaching the peasants basic agricultural and other techniques. Such a campaign, said CELU, could only take place when a people's government was established, and the basic problems of development tackled.

It was quite a challenge to the new military rulers – and they reacted the following morning by issuing a bitter attack on the CELU leaders, accusing them of trying to sabotage the revolutionary movement.

Already the military were finding that it was easier to overthrow a regime than to build one, and from this point on the quality of their propaganda began to deteriorate, and their statements to take on more desperate and repressive tones.

A further statement against CELU the following day included a series of phrases and comments about enemies of the revolution 'working with foreign elements' and about 'criminal plots of reactionaries' and references to 'imperialist agents' which gave a clue to the direction of the new movement, which was to show increasing signs of selective xenophobia and anti-Western bias.

World opinion had been almost entirely concerned with the fate of the deposed Emperor, and offers of asylum had come from Cameroon, Gabon and, unofficially, from friends in Britain.

Even countries sympathetic to the military regime cautioned the new rulers to deal gently with the 'old man of Africa'. The mood was summed up pretty well in the *New Nigerian*: 'Even at this moment of crisis, Haile Selassie deserves a sympathetic appreciation for preserving the independence of his country against the Italian fascists who attempted to colonize Ethiopia. On the African scene, Haile Selassie's role as a mediator and a founding father of the OAU is well known.'

On September 20, the new head of the military government, General Aman (whose exact role was still not clear) held a press conference, the main point of which was to announce that any decision on whether Ethiopia would become a republic would be left 'to the people to decide'. Exactly *how* and *when* they would decide was not made clear.

It was an impressive performance, nevertheless. The distinguished fifty-year-old General stood in front of the dust-sheet-covered throne so recently vacated by Haile Selassie, in the richly-tapestried Audience Room of the Grand Palace, and in impeccable English parried awkward questions like an experienced politician. He might only be, officially, the 'spokesman' of the new government, but he looked and talked like a man tk be reckoned with.

He declined to reveal the whereabouts of the deposed Emperor, but disclosed that Haile Selassie was still refusing to give up the government funds the military claimed he had put in foreign banks. The question of the Emperor's being put on trial, he said, was 'premature as were questions about Ethiopia being declared a republic, and the duration of the 'provisional' nature of the military government. But the detained ministers and officials *would* be tried by court martial. He also revealed officially for the first time that the Dergue consisted of 120 men, none above the rank of major, and hinted at a peaceful solution to the problems in Eritrea.

Two days later the PMAC issued details of its proposed 'Civilian Advisory Body', which included representatives from the farmers, teachers, the Church, and commerce, as well as one from each ministry and one from each of the country's fourteen provincial administrations. Its functions would be to draft administrative procedures for the new people's government which would be elected at some later date, to draft a new constitution based on 'Ethiopia First' and to study and propose social, economic and political reforms.

The new thirty-one man body also included three members of CELU. But the labour leaders were not to be won over so easily. On Monday, September 23 representatives of the Dergue went to CELU and demanded that they retract their statement attacking the military government. The labour leaders refused. That afternoon jeeps arrived at the CELU headquarters near Mexico Square and forcibly removed the organization's three top men.

As the word spread, university students, who were due to start registering for the new session that day, refused to enter the campus, and hung around in groups outside. Inside, other members of the Dergue were meeting with the University Lecturers' Association — amd emerged with a statement from the lecturers that they supported the military government and its campaign to send them and the students into the countryside to take part in the crash rural education programme, otherwise known as the National Work Campaign or 'Zemecha'. The students had meantime decided they would *not* take part.

Next day, however, what was left of the CELU leadership called for a general strike to start the following day, Wednesday.

110

It was almost totally ignored. A few employees at the Ministry of Finance came out – although the Dergue denied it at the time. But otherwise everyone carried on as usual. It was less support for the military, however, then fear of reprisals that won the day. As one trader put it: 'I don't know what's going on – and I'm not taking any chances. Why should I get myself shot?' It was a severe blow to CELU, which in the closing weeks of Haile Selassie's reign had begun to feel it had some power after all.

Maskal '74 – Hamlet Without The Prince (September 26-27)

On September 26 the Military Council announced that it had abolished the historical claim of Ethiopian kings to rule by divine right. They also abolished what they called the 'embarrassing and pretentious' titles used by Haile Selassie. Future kings might call themselves the 'Lion of Ethiopia', but there was to be no reference to being 'Elect of God' or to being descended from the tribe of Judah. Provincial Governors General would in future be known simply as 'Administrators'.

The statement had been timed for maximum effect on the population, which that day started a weekend of celebrations – called Maskal – which in Ethiopian church lore marked the finding of the 'true cross'. It was an event which traditionally involved the Emperor himself and normally outshone all other Ethiopian festivals, including Christmas, New Year and Easter, for pomp, ceremony and colour. It was the Emperor's 'day' – and Haile Selassie – flanked by his lions on chain leads – normally led a huge procession of his ministers and nobles and retainers through the streets of Addis to Maskal Square, where a huge bonfire was lit at dusk on the 27th – Maskal Day. The Emperor himself, surrounded by colourfully-dressed chanting priests swinging censers, lit the bonfire, and tens of thousands gathered to cheer.

Maskal 1974, however, was obviously going to be different. In fact, it almost didn't happen at all. The military were afraid of public demonstrations, and had told the city fathers in Addis that there would be no Maskal parade and no bonfire. The civic leaders

111

were horrified, and after days of argument, the military relented.

At 2 pm on the afternoon of the 27th the radio announced that there would be a Maskal bonfire after all, and by 5 pm thousands of people had gathered in the square round the hastily-built bonfire – a crowd which was only a little smaller than usual. It was carefully marshalled by hundreds of soldiers and police. It had been agreed that the Emperor's role of fire-lighter would *not* be taken by anyone in uniform. Instead, the acting mayor of Addis was asked to perform the almost holy task.

The crowds dispersed quietly afterwards without incident. A few hundred stayed on into the darkness to see what happened to the bonfire, however. For legend ran that if it fell toward the Palace, it would be a good year, and if it fell the other way, a bad one. In fact, the fire collapsed in on itself, inconclusively. Which just about summed up what was about to happen to the country.

De-Selassination – And Division (September 28 - November 22)

The success of Maskal, as far as the new military rulers were concerned, ushered in a period of consolidation for the Dergue – to outward appearances at least.

Attacks on the old regime, and particularly on the ex-Emperor, continued in the press. The Haile Selassie Theatre was re-named the National Theatre, and the words 'Imperial' and 'Haile Selassie' began to be erased from official documents, although paradoxically, new money and new postage stamps appeared still bearing the picture of the Emperor.

On October 5, the military were able to announce that the Airborne Division Commander, Colonel Alem-Zewd Tessema, had 'surrendered'. The announcement said he had been 'used by the former officials to create division between the Air Force and the Airborne Division'.

On October 7, however, there was an incident which suggested that all was not as well within the military as the PMAC would have people believe. There had been murmurings within the Army

Engineering Corps and the Airborne Division that a small group of officers on the Dergue seemed to have too much say in events, and that there should be a speedy return to civilian rule.

It seems likely that friends of Colonel Alem-Zewd had something to do with the anti-Dergue move. The Dergue ordered the dissidents of the Engineering Corps to surrender. They refused. The military rulers then ordered the rest of the Corps to arrest the ringleaders of this 'rebellion' and hand them over. Again there was a refusal. So representatives of the Dergue — with a heavy guard — went to the Engineering Corps HQ where engineers and members of the Airborne Division were holding a mass meeting. When the officers of the Co-ordinating Committee entered and demanded that the dissidents be handed over, a group of engineers attacked them. In the ensuing fight five died and seven were wounded.

Meantime the military continued to arrest 'reactionaries' and 'dissidents' — many, within the military themselves, never to be admitted officially — and various steps were taken to wipe out the remnants of the old regime.

Goodwill missions were sent round to neighbouring countries, and a competition was announced for a new national anthem to replace the one proclaiming 'O Ethiopia be happy, by God's power and your Emperor'.

On October 24, General Aman announced that the people of Ethiopia would be given an opportunity to decide on the future of the monarchy by referendum. The idea of designating the Crown Prince as King had been 'only a temporary measure'.

In fact it was a period of rising expectations, and apart from the brief gunbattle with the Engineering Corps, of relative outward calm.

Continuing their programme of ridding the country of Haile Selassie's influence the PMAC announced, not surprisingly, that the public holidays celebrating his coronation and his birthday were henceforth cancelled. And on October 28 they announced that a grandson of the ex-Emperor's, twenty-four-year-old Lt. Prince Makonnen, had been dishonourably discharged from the army. He had refused to return from advanced training in the United States.

At the same time another 'royal' was declared an outlaw – Ras Mengesha Seyoum, great-grandson of Emperor Yohannes of Tigre. Ras Mengesha, whose wife, Aida, a grand-daughter of Haile Selassie, was in detention in Addis along with other members of the royal family, had disappeared into the countryside shortly after the Emperor was deposed – although he had never been a supporter of Haile Selassie, and had, in fact, been regarded as a progressive. Ras Mengesha was considered to be the most serious threat – after the Eritrean situation – to the new regime.

Meanwhile, the papers continued to be full of long essays, tinged with Marxist and Maoist rhetoric, on the meaning of 'Ethiopia First'. The PMAC moved its headquarters from the Fourth Army Division Headquarters and took over the Grand Palace, taking Haile Selassie with them.

In the cellars of this same palace more than two hundred ministers, officials and military figures – some of whom had been detained since April – still awaited their fate, and early in November attention turned again to them with the publication of the report of the Commission of Inquiry into Corruption in connection with its investigation of the Wollo drought. The Commission indicted thirty-five people, some for failing to discharge adequately their personal responsibilities, others for collective responsibility for the tragedy. (My 'prophet', who had predicted that Professor Mesfin would not survive as chairman, had been proved right – and the chairmanship had been taken over by an appointee of the Dergue, Lt.-Com. Lemma Gutema of the Navy.)

Two special courts were set up by proclamation to try those indicted, and the military's statement pointed out that in order to implement the motto of 'Ethiopia First' it had 'been found necessary to provide efficient, speedy and decisive machinery of justice'. Just how speedy and decisive we were soon to find out.

Simultaneously with this announcement, two things happened which were obviously connected with each other, and with the proclamation concerning the detainees and their trials, although the latter connection was not immediately apparent.

The first was a rumour that General Aman was about to resign.

The second, on November 18, was an official statement disclosing the identity of the First Vice-Chairman of the PMAC as Major Mengistu Haile Mariam. It was also revealed that he was the true head of the 'Executive Committee' of the Military Council.

The announcement coincided with a series of rallies which should have been addressed by General Aman, but which were attended instead by Major Mengistu and other members of the PMAC. In a speech on Friday, November 22 Major Mengistu covered predictable ground in denouncing the Haile Selassie regime, promising priority treatment for land reform and urging every Ethiopian to play his part. But several aspects of the address were vastly different from the speeches that had become the norm.

He warned students who had been expressing opposition to the National Work Campaign that they had better change their attitude 'rapidly'. He referred to Eritrean rebels who with foreign backing had been disturbing the peace for thirteen years — somewhat less conciliatory language than General Aman had used.

And, most significant of all, he warned sharply that the PMAC was 'bedevilled by reactionaries elected to the highest position of responsibility within the movement'.

10 The Shattered Dream

Fateful Friday (November 22)

About lunchtime on Friday, November 22 Reuters correspondent John Talbot received a mysterious phone call asking him to go immediately to General Aman Andom's home in the grounds of the Princess Tsehai Hospital. He went – but Mengistu's soldiers had got there first. As John's car drove into the hospital compound, soldiers waving sub-machine-guns stopped him.

He spent the next three and a half hours in the Fourth Division HQ explaining away his presence at the General's house.

Back at his city centre house-cum-office his wife received another cryptic phone call. It informed her that the armed forces had arrested 'that one-eyed Englishman who works for you' – a reference to John's black eyepatch, a legacy from other, harsher days elsewhere. But he had been in the hospital grounds long enough to establish one fact – General Aman was under house arrest.

There had been a strong rumour of this all week, and since the previous weekend the General had not been seen outside his house. But the story had started weeks before, on the very day Haile Selassie had been deposed.

True, the Armed Forces Co-ordinating Committee had developed into a democratic organization. Its 120 members were drawn equally from all units of the armed forces and police. They were split into a number of sub-committees with special responsibilities – for the economy, internal security, foreign affairs,

116

social reforms and agricultural reform. The chairmanship of the full committee had been rotated among the chairmen of these various Revolutionary Sub-committees, and decisions had been arrived at after debate and by majority vote.

But gradually one person had taken the chair of the full committee more often than any other — Major Mengistu. He emerged as a hard-liner; a tough little soldier, he was a half-caste Galla of negroid appearance, unlike the usually finer-featured Ethiopians who use the derogatory description 'shankalla' (a term approximating to nigger) of black Africans. Little is yet known of his background, except that he served in the Third Division at Harar and that he was strongly left-wing and eastward-looking in his politics. He had gradually gathered round himself a group of like-minded men who formed the 'Executive Council' or 'Inner' Dergue, and by mid-November this group had taken control of the Armed Forces Co-ordinating Committee and were dictating events.

However, he was also shrewd enough to realize that, for some at least, the revolution needed a moderate front. And preferably a popular figure. Hence the choice of Aman Andom, whose close associations with the Third Division must have brought him into contact with Mengistu at some stage. Like Michael Imru before him, however, General Aman, hero of Korea and the Somali front — where he earned the affectionate nickname 'The Desert Lion', sound family man and churchgoer, was not the man to play puppet.

From the start he insisted not only on being *called* chairman of the Co-ordinating Committee, but on actually holding the position. The ensuing conflict had caused the initial confusion over his titles.

Three things had proved Aman's undoing as far as Major Mengistu and his small group of committed extremists on the Dergue were concerned, however. The first came a few weeks after his appointment when he showed reluctance to give up any of his positions, and there may be some truth in the claim made later that General Aman had become to see himself in the rmle of first president of the Republic of Ethiopia.

The second red rag to the bull-necked Mengistu was Aman's approach to Eritrea. The General, being an Eritrean, genuinely

117

wanted a peaceful solution and was prepared to negotiate with the ELF. Mengistu not only did not share this view, but was determined to wipe out all secessionist elements in the province.

Thirdly, Mengistu was convinced that the revolution would not be complete until the symbols of the old regime – the ministers, generals and officials now in detention – were executed. Formal trials, with the risk that someone might escape what he considered to be justice, were both soft and dangerous. During the weekend of November 17 Mengistu's group had presented General Aman with two demands. One was for authorization to send additional troops to Eritrea for a major offensive against the ELF. The other was for his signature to a list of detainees to be executed by firing squad. (Since the General was still at least nominally head of the government, his signature was legally necessary.)

General Aman refused on both counts. He still believed no lasting solution could be found to the Eritrean problem by using force. He was equally determined that, however rigged people might believe them to be, trials of the detainees had to be held if the military government was to keep faith with the Ethiopian people and avoid the condemnation of the world. He was a soldier. He was the head of a revolutionary military government. But he was also a Christian.

When Major Mengistu indicated that he would go ahead anyway, General Aman said he would have nothing more to do ith the regime. In effect he had resigned, but either believing that not even Mengistu would go through with this plan, or that saner counsels in the Dergue would prevail, instead of publicly resigning the General sat at home and waited for developments. By midweek he had been joined by a number of loyal officers and men and had sent word to his former command, the Third Division in Harar, for support. For reasons that can only be guessed at, the message appears not to have got through.

During that week, as he watched the emergence into the public eye of Major Mengistu, and the apparent acquiescence of the rest of the Dergue, Aman realized that the next step would almost certainly

118

be a demand that he give himself up. He told a friend: 'I will never surrender to these men. I would rather kill myself.'

On Friday morning Major Mengistu decided it was time to make his move. There was just one problem – the air force. Many of the air force radicals who had been so active in propelling the revolution along to its September 12 climax, had since been critical of the establishment of a military government. They genuinely wanted to hand power back to the civilians quickly. Also it was largely composed of Eritreans and Tigreans; therefore, before going to the mass rally on November 22 where he made his reference to 'PMAC reactionaries', the Major went to Debre Zeit and called the airmen together. After considerable argument he persuaded them not to resist any moves against General Aman.

In the afternoon, shortly after Major Mengistu's statement about reactionaries in the Dergue, troops were seen parking jeeps outside the compound of the Princess Tsehai Hospital, with machine guns pointing at the General's home. That evening, thanks to John Talbot, the truth of Amam's predicament was public knowledge.

Bloody Saturday (November 23-24)

On the morning of Saturday, November 23 neither *The Ethiopian Herald* nor Radio Ethiopia made any mention of what was happening around General Aman's home. The tension mounted throughout the day, with more troops surrounding the General's house, and soldiers posted at the roadside to discourage people from stopping to look at what was going on.

At 8 o'clock that evening as I drove past the General's house on my way to the telex office, more jeeps mounted with 15-millimetre machine-guns were arriving, and a group of officers appeared to be holding a meeting just outside the hospital compound.

I was on the point of completing transmission of a round-up story to *The Observer* when my wife telephoned to give me two items of news – firstly, that the radio had just announced that General Aman had been removed from his post as head of the PMAC 'because he refused to cooperate with the Armed Forces'. And secondly that from her vantage point overlooking the south side of the city she could hear gunfire and explosions.

I quickly tagged the information onto the end of my *Observer* piece, sent a newsflash item to the BBC and *Sunday Express,* booked a call to ABC in New York and, with the irrepressible John Talbot, went back up the Jimma Road to the scene of the fighting. There was obviously a lull and we drove past, turned round and came back. There were plenty of troops around, but no firing. Again I slowed down, but when some soldiers waving sub-machine-guns started to come towards us, we beat a hasty retreat.

The military statement announcing the removal of Aman Andom had accused him of making appointments without consulting the Dergue, and of showing a 'dictatorial attitude'. He was also accused of trying to split the armed forces by making secret arrangements with some units, and of lacking decisive leadership.

Well into the small hours of Sunday morning the normal sounds of Addis by night – barking dogs and the occasional howl of a hyena – were interrupted by the sound of gunfire. On Sunday morning Radio Ethiopia announced that sixty persons had been executed by order of the PMAC 'for crimes against the Ethiopian people'. The executions had taken place in the courtyard of the main civil prison, Akaki jail. Among the list of dead read out on the radio were two former Premiers, Aklilu Habte Wold and Lij Endalkatchew Makonnen; Haile Selassie's grandson, Rear Admiral Eskinder Desta; two of the country's top noblemen, Ras Asrate Kassa and Ras Mesfin Shileshi; two former Defence Ministers, Lt.-General Abiye Abebe and Lt.-General Kebede Gebre; the ex-Information Minister Dr. Tesfay Gebre-Egzy and one of his two assistants, Tegegne Yetashework; Aklilu's brother, Akale-Work Habte Wold; Colonel Solomon Kedir, the former head of security; Lt.-General Yilma Shibeshi, the former Police Chief; Lt.-General Assefa Ayene, former Air Force Commander, Army Chief of Staff and Minister of Posts; and Colonel Alem-Zewd Tessema. The list of military figures also included Lt.-Generals Deresse Dubale, Haile Baikedagne, Assefa Demissie (the Emperor's ADC), and Debebe Haile-Mariam (Governor of Eritrea); Maj.-Generals Seyoum Gedle

Giorghis, ex-Commander of the Second Division, and Tafessa Lemma, Commander of the Imperial Bodyguard.

The list also included the name, almost at the end, of General Aman Andom. It was three days before the Dergue admitted that General Aman had died in a gun-battle and had not been executed along with the others.

Anyone driving through the city that morning who hadn't heard the news would have had no indication that anything unusual had happened. Troops were stopping and diverting traffic on the roads approaching Akaki jail, but elsewhere in the city life appeared to be going on normally.

Underneath, however, most people were stunned. Executions of some of the detainees had been expected, even urged by many citizens. But dragging people in front of firing squads in the middle of the night was not the Ethiopian way of justice. And the biggest blow of all was the news of Aman Andom's death. One acquaintance of mine who had often commented that if it were up to him, the Emperor would be 'taken out and hung three times in the market place', was dejected. 'The others – yes,' he said, 'but they have made a big mistake killing General Aman.'

Only a few teenagers – not students – seemed pleased. 'This is what we have been waiting for,' said one. 'They had it coming – now the revolution can really begin.'

That afternoon groups of women, shrouded in the jet-black dresses and shawls of mourners, shuffled round parts of the Ethiopian capital wailing and singing. Every now and then they would go into a shuttered house for a while and sit down and weep a little with the family who lived there. Then, joined by members of that family, they would go on to the next house.

It was not an unfamiliar sight in Addis Ababa. It is the traditional way families pay respect to their dead and the dead of their friends. But on this Sunday, these women were defying tradition. For their loved ones had died the death of traitors and criminals, their bodies placed in unmarked graves. No one was allowed to ask for the remains, and no public mourning was permitted. But for these women whose husbands had died without benefit of open trial in a night of madness, it was a gesture – futile, perhaps, but brave.

In the meantime, we began to piece together the truth behind the events of that night of tragedy, in which some of the best political, military and administrative brains and the cream of the aristocracy in Ethiopia were wiped out.

Just before 8 pm on the Saturday evening, a truck-load of troops had driven into the hospital grounds and drawn up in front of General Aman's house. Through a megaphone, an order was given for the General to surrender peacefully within five minutes or the soldiers would open fire. As the last seconds ticked away, a shot was fired from inside the house – and all hell broke loose. It was soon obvious that rifles and machine-guns were making little impression on the thick-walled house; a tank was brought in to smash down a corner of the building – and the machine-guns did the rest.

In the middle of the fighting, however, another order was given – to send other units of the Fourth Division at the Grand Palace to transfer a number of prisoners to Akaki jail for execution by firing squad. Again, no one knows who actually gave the order, though Major Mengistu certainly ratified it and it was widely believed it was his idea, probably for two reasons. First and foremost it seems likely that even the Major did not imagine that General Aman would put up such a fight, and probably expected to be able to take him alive. Aman could then have been denounced for a few days, and executed along with several others whose names the Dergue had already agreed would be at the top of the list. (By this time – within the Dergue at least – the Major had abandoned all pretence at anything but the most summary hearings before killing the prisoners.) He was aware however, that while the execution, even without trial, of people like Aklilu Habte Wold and some of the former ministers and officials might be accepted, there could be a strong reaction to the death of General Aman, particularly within the armed forces. By hurriedly bringing the executions forward to that night, he would split and confuse his potential opponents and diffuse the impact of Aman's death – and indeed in this he was to prove successful.

The second reason suggested is that the act of executing the prisoners would help 'unite' the Dergue as never before. It would be an act of commitment, from which it would be difficult for any members of the Co-ordinating Committee to back down.

In the event, elements of both reasons, coupled with panic, probably combined to produce the fateful decision.

Most of the prisoners were still all together in the main cellars beneath the Banqueting Hall. While the battle was still raging round Aman's house, soldiers went to the cellars and read off a list of names. This list is believed to have originally consisted of only six names — the six 'key' figures whose executions Aman Andom had refused to sanction — the two ex-Premiers, Eskinder Desta, Ras Asrate, Ras Mesfin and General Abiye. But another fifty-three names were called out. The detainees were told they were going for further interrogation. It must have seemed an odd time — if indeed the prisoners were aware of the time — but some certainly appeared to believe the story. When they failed to return within a few hours, those left behind began to suspect the worst.

As well as those transported in trucks to Akaki jail at least two were brought from a military hospital on stretchers — Blatta Admassu, the Emperor's treasurer, and Lt.-General Esayas Gebre Selassie, a Senator who had previously been Chief of Staff of the Emperor's private cabinet.

Sometimes singly, sometimes in batches of two or three, the prisoners were taken into the courtyard and shot. Some reports say Blatta Admassu remained unconscious throughout and had to be propped up in a chair to be shot. Ras Asrate Kassa was said to have been shot sitting in a wheelchair. Some of the men screamed and shouted abuse at their executioners. Others stood calm and dignified. All were buried in a mass, unmarked grave in the prison grounds.

Having cut off one head by deposing Haile Selassie, Ethiopia's revolutionaries had been given a chance — unbelievable at the beginning of 1974 — to grow a new one in the form, however nominal, of Aman Andom. He at least had the appearance and makings of a unifying force. Now that head, too, had been cut off. The executions of the fifty-nine ministers, officials, generals and nobles – almost an entire generation of leaders – had also been a form of decapitation.

When Crown Councillor Abebe Retta had been led out to the firing squad he had pointed a finger at his executioners and told them: 'You will never rule Ethiopia this way. For you don't understand your own country, and you don't know your own people.' Whether they did or not still remains, at the time of writing, to be seen.

The New Puppet (November 24-29)

In a lengthy statement on Sunday, November 24 the Dergue attempted to justify their action by calling it 'an important political decision in accordance with the pledge given to the Ethiopian people to punish all those responsible for the misery of the masses through abuse of authority, maladministration and judicial malpractices'.

But world reaction was almost unanimous in condemning the 'outrage'. At the United Nations, African states put forward a resolution, carried unanimously, calling on the Ethiopian Military Council to spare the life of Haile Selassie and the lives of the others in detention. The United States suspended military aid. And Crown Prince Asfa Wossen – still king-designate – condemned 'unproductive vengeance'. Meanwhile the world's press was also united in its condemnation – the most outspoken being the media in other African states.

The *Times of Zambia* talked of 'cold-blooded murders', adding that the executions were 'the most dastardly savagery ever committed in the name of revolution, justice, democracy or whatever else the soldiers in Addis Ababa profess to believe in. It rivals the liquidation of leading Ugandans by Idi Amin ... is reminiscent of the Congo ... it is another huge blot on the history of this continent.'

In the Zambian paper's comments was a clue to the sense of outrage felt throughout Africa. For Ethiopia's revolution *had* until then been relatively bloodless. It *had* been unique, certainly in a

124

continent where changes of government come oftener via the bullet than the ballot box. And Africans were *proud* of the Ethiopian revolution, seeing in it an example to the world of a civilized coup. And 'Bloody Saturday' had shattered this image.

The Ethiopian Herald, meantime, carried an unrepentant editorial saying that the executions should 'serve as a lesson to succeeding generations of Ethiopians'.

The fate of the Emperor was uppermost in many minds, of course, and rumours emanating from Beirut that he was also to be executed were angrily and officially denied by the PMAC.

The same day, November 27, the ELF leader in Beirut, Osman Saleh Sabbi issued a statement claiming that the military rulers in Ethiopia were planning a 'major escalation' of the conflict in the north. But, he warned, the ELF had arms and money supplied by Arab sympathizers, and were prepared to fight.

In fact, even as he was speaking, five thousand extra troops were on their way north from Addis Ababa. On November 28 this was confirmed in a statement from the PMAC, published in the Eritrean press, denying that the extra troops had been sent to 'massacre the population'. They had been sent 'to improve security'.

Later the same day the PMAC issued a strongly-worded reply to an attack by the Ugandan President, General Idi Amin, on Ethiopia's military rulers for the Saturday evening massacre. General Amin had offered asylum to refugees from Ethiopia and particularly to the deposed Emperor. In their reply, the PMAC accused the Ugandan President of trying to 'subvert African unity' and added: 'In any case, people who live in glass houses shouldn't throw stones.' Which was at least fair comment!

That evening, the PMAC announced the appointment of a new Chairman to replace General Aman Andom. It was the Commander of the Second Division, Brigadier-General Teferi Benti. At the swearing-in ceremony, the First Vice Chairman of the Co-ordinating Committee, Major Mengistu, said they had chosen the fifty-three-year-old General because of his 'exemplary conduct and the high qualities of leadership he has always displayed'. The description was not believed to quite fit the facts. For according to

125

some reports, General Teferi had been in the United States at the start of the revolt in February on a military course, and had been described at the end of it as a man with no leadership potential.

In any event, what Major Mengistu didn't say was that General Teferi had been their second choice. The first man they approached to take over the Chairman's post had been the enigmatic Commander of the Territorial Army, Lt.-General Jagema Kelo, the country's leading Galla chieftain. General Jagema, however, was on the point of retiring and declined on the grounds of poor health.

Black Monday (November 30 – December 3)

How to get their hands on the Emperor's money had been a major preoccupation of the Dergue prior to the events of Bloody Saturday, and they soon returned to the theme. All the experts said that if Haile Selassie had money in Switzerland, that was probably the last anyone would ever see of it – unless he took it out himself. But on November 30 Radio Ethiopia announced that the 'former king' had signed a letter 'of his own free will' agreeing to transfer 'all his personal and family fortunes and financial holdings in local and foreign banks to the Drought Relief and Rehabilitation Commission' in Ethiopia.

The official text of the PMAC's statement added: 'The former Emperor did not say where his fortunes were being kept nor how much they were worth. However the PMAC is sparing no effort to find out the exact amount of these fortunes and where they are'. In other words, Haile Selassie had in effect told them. 'You can have my money – if you can find it!'

On the evening of the 30th, some friends were coming away from the restaurant at the international airport when there was a loud explosion nearby. Within minutes they and about thirty others – several foreign nationals among them – were detained by soldiers who were rushing about 'in a state of panic', as one eyewitness put it. (Some were released the following day but most were kept in police headquarters cells for several days.) The explosion had been caused by a bomb apparently thrown from a car into the aircraft fuel dump. Fortunately, it didn't reach the main tanks, but it was enough to cause a major alert throughout the city and guards were doubled on the radio stations and public buildings.

On the following Monday morning, December 2, Bill Lee and I were sitting in my home overlooking the city, discussing the Saturday evening explosion. There was speculation that it was the work of an Eritrean separatist guerilla group which was believed to have come into the city the previous week, and we discussed the likelihood of a wave of bombings. Prime target, we decided, would almost certainly be the impressive city hall, which stands on a hill in the centre of the city, its clock tower reaching up into the sky. A few minutes later, we heard a loud explosion. Bill leapt up. 'My God – they've blown up the city hall,' he shouted. Even as we watched there was another billow of smoke and a second explosion.

Stopping only to grab a camera and tape recorder, we dashed into the city, taking a short cut through some back streets. Had we not done so we might well have been caught in yet another explosion along the main road, which blasted out the reception area and part of the centre block of the Wabe Shebelle Hotel.

The scene round the city hall – known as the Municipality – was incredible. Part of one wing had had a huge hole blown in it from one side right through to the other. Tangled window frames and concrete lay around the courtyard and hung in grotesque shapes from the side of the building. Thousands of people were milling around, oblivious to the possible danger of more explosions, and troops and police seemed as stunned as everyone else.

I snatched some pictures of the damage and then – after a brief stop at the telex room to file a newsflash tk the BBC – we headed for the Wabe Shebelle Hotel to see if reports of the explosion there were true. They were. The whole frontage of the central block, including the reception area, had been blown thirty yards across the road, and the first floor had collapsed. Windows all round had been smashed and broken glass was everywhere.

Road blocks had been set up some distance from the hotel, but seeing our government press cards an officer allowed us through to look at the damage close-to and take some pictures. As we finished

127

and turned to walk away, a crowd of civilians, mainly the young people who are never far away from an 'incident' in Addis, began to shout abuse at us, calling us 'CIA pigs'. It was a cry we had heard before from such groups. But when stones began to come our way we quickened our pace. Within seconds we were being chased by a howling, stone-throwing mob.

Suddenly, as I turned to see if they were gaining on us, I saw some riot police running with the crowd and waving and shouting to us to stop. We did, thinking we would be able to explain to them what had happened and show them our credentials.

We spent the next few minutes fighting off the crowd — some trying to take our wallets and my camera equipment — and being pummelled and kicked by the riot police. Finally police reinforcements arrived and made the civilian mob stand back. We tried to explain the situation, and waved our government press passes. But in vain. The police continued to push and jostle us, one viciously tsisting Bill's arm behind him and grabbing the back of his hair. Another did the same to me — then let go my hair and pulled his pistol. He put the barrel to my temple and told me to move. I moved; but gently. That hundred yards or so over rough ground with an angry mob in tow and a nervous policeman's gun at my temple was the longest walk of my life.

We were eventually handed over to a major outside the Wabe Shebelle. He spoke perfect English, was sympathetic, but had orders to detain anyone acting suspiciously. I explained why we had run away. He understood — but orders were orders. If we could get someone to vouch for us we would probably be released. Altogether, about twenty foreign journalists were arrested in various parts of the city that day, and it took embassies well into the evening to trace them all, mainly because telephone services seemed mysteriously out of order.

To cut a long story short, for the rest of that day we were hustled about between the army and the police. Neither knew what to do with us since they knew we had broken no laws. But they were equally afraid of the wrath of their superior officers and were erring on the side of caution. Finally, about 7 o'clock, a young regular police officer took our names and addresses and said he would accept responsibility for releasing us.

By the time I caught up with events next day – a day which included some frantic diplomatic exchanges between the Foreign Office in London and the British Embassy in Addis, resulting from a chance spotting by those I worked for at the BBC and *Daily Express* of a report of my arrest in the *Daily Telegraph* – the official toll was two dead and thirteen injured. The figures were, and are, treated with some scepticism.

The immediate result of the bombings was a wave of new arrests, officially justified on the grounds that these were relatives and supporters of some of those who had been executed. But it was noticed that everyone detained was an Eritrean.

That night, December 3, the PMAC calmly announced that the public was 'not to be worried by the sound of firearms from time to time while security men rounded up reactionaries and enemies of the people'!

'Peace and Tranquillity' (December 4-11)
Ethiopia emerged from its two weeks of death, destruction and detentions with a great deal of apprehension – and without a Foreign Minister. Dejazmatch Zewde Gebre Selassie, who had survived from the beginning of the Endalkatchew administration, had been in New York for the United Nations General Assembly when the executions took place, and he had sent word that he would not be returning. The post was given to Kifle Wodajo, a former Ambassador to Washington, on December 6.

A few days later the military announced the start of the long-awaited – and for at least fifty-nine people rather belated – trials of former ministers and officials. In fact, the brief public hearings were a farce, with unknown figures appearing in the dock on relatively minor charges. On the opening day, December 10, the hearings were adjourned after only half an hour. The real trials were believed to be going on in secret, but there was no indication as to who the defendants were or what charges they were facing.

129

Coincident with the opening of the trials – and to the more cynical observers, as an explanation of why they were being held at all – the new PMAC Chairman, General Teferi, sent a message to the United Nations in reply to Secretary-General Kurt Woldheim's telegram following the executions. General Teferi said the UN's appeal had been 'somewhat speculative' as far as the Council's future actions were concerned and had been 'based on erronous assumptions and false and malicious newspaper reports'. The message assured the UN that all the remaining prisoners were being well fed, well clothed and enjoying privileges not shared by prisoners in many other countries. The message, however, made no reference at all to the executions.

The following day, December 11, General Teferi Benti held his first press conference. (His name had in the past few days officially undergone a metamorphosis to its Amharic version of Teferi Bante, presumably to disguise his Galla origins and quell the growing rumours – assisted by the introduction of Galligna broadcasts on Radio Ethiopia – that the revolution was now controlled by the Gallas.)

Unlike his predecessor, General Teferi conducted the press conference in Amharic. He explained that the executions had been carried out because the PMAC wanted to be honest to themselves and to world opinion. Otherwise, he said, 'we would have conducted mock trials'. The prisoners who had been executed he explained, had been plotting with General Aman to crush the revolution. The General was obviously ill at ease in his new role, and when he replied to a question about the fate of the deposed Emperor he referred to Haile Selassie as 'His Imperial Majesty'. The faux pas was not lost on the Ethiopians and the few foreign journalists who knew the language. The interpreter – a man who had played the same role on many occasions for the deposed Emperor – blandly translated this phrase as 'the deposed King'. But the point of the answer was that Haile Selassie had 'committed crimes against the Ethiopian people. There is no question of exile for him.' If the people desired it, he would be put on trial.

It was during this press conference that the General made a

comment that was to be turned into a kind of catchphrase: 'Even during this critical period, all of you have noticed that there was peace in the country and life was going on normally.' The state media were to pick up and repeat the idea of 'peace and tranquillity'.

Ethiopia First = Socialism (December 12-17)

More and more articles on socialism in Soviet countries and the progress of the Chinese revolution had been appearing in the press since the overthrow of the Emperor, and in particular in the early weeks of December. Thus it was no surprise when, on December 13, the Military Council virtually declared Ethiopia a socialist state. The country would be run by a 'Supreme Progressive Council', a one-party system would be established, all villages would be formed into people's communes and co-operative farms would be set up. The statement added that all economic activity would be brought under state control, with the exception of a few private businesses, and hinted broadly at the total nationalization of land.

Reaction in the capital was mixed. The business community – Ethiopian and foreign-owned – was apprehensive to say the least, but the students and CELU appeared to welcome the news. The big question was how the rural population would react to land nationalization, communes and cooperatives. Obviously in those parts of the country – notably the southern Galla lands – where most of the land was owned by wealthy Amharas, the news would be welcome. But in the west and north where people generally tended their own small patches of land, and where the bigger landowners still had the loyalty of the people who worked for them, the measures were expected to meet with resistance.

Land nationalization would also hit hard the country's biggest single landowner – the Ethiopian Orthodox Church. The Church's ineffectiveness in support of Haile Selassie suggested it would not be able to muster strong opposition, but it might prove another source of discontent.

At any event, it was one thing to announce such measures. It

131

would be quite another to implement them among people who had a long history of resistance to interference from central government.

The PMAC's statement came on the eve of a mass rally and parade in Addis Ababa to launch the National Work Campaign or 'Zemecha'. The authorities claimed some 60,000 students and young people would take part. But it was known that thousands of students – particularly from the north – had refused to register for the Zemecha, and many who had registered had, at the last moment, decided to disappear into the countryside.

The parade on Saturday, December 14, however, was still an impressive occasion, as some 20,000 students, in their light khaki uniforms and Cuban-style revolutionary caps marched in formation through the city, followed by the buses and trucks which would, over the next few weeks, take them and their equipment and supplies into all parts of the countryside.

The day also provided further proof of General Teferi's secondary role. At the rally in Jan Hoy Meda, the city's main sports field and race course, the salute at the march past had been taken by the General, flanked by Major Mengistu and his Second Vice Chairman, Major Atanafu Abate, a man who was appearing more and more on the scene, who had spent some time in China during his military training, and who was believed to be the force now pushing the revolution decidely to the left. As the last of the marchers took up their position for the parade through the city, General Teferi and Major Mengistu, sitting side by side in the back of an open jeep, went to the head of the parade.

Thousands of people lined the route, and as they cheered, the smiling, bespectacled and rather benign-looking General started to respond with a genteel 'royal' wave. After a few minutes, however, the shouts and cheers of the crowd became one dominant and distinguishable cry – 'Mengistu, Mengistu!'

The General looked decidedly embarrassed. Slowly, he lowered his waving arm and for the rest of the journey sat disconsolately in the jeep while Major Mengistu, responding to the calls, became more animated and soon started waving first one, then both hands.

The incident, and its effect on Major Mengistu, was to produce more problems within the Dergue.

The military rulers ended their first hundred days in power with little to show other than a mass grave, some badly damaged buildings, and growing civilian unrest over the lack of progress. The people didn't want declarations and explanations of socialism — a word for which there was no exact equivalent in Amharic anyway. (The phrase used in Amharic — 'hibrette sebawinet' — was being variously interpreted by Ethiopians as anything from 'humanism' to 'community of the people'.)

What was wanted, for example, was the fifty cents a day pay rise for manual workers promised in March and still not implemented, and a fairer deal for the peasants. They no longer had to give seventy-five per cent of their crops to feudal landlords, but to the state. Individually, they were no better off.

If anyone had any doubts as to the direction of, and influence on, the new military rulers, the fuss created by the arrival of a new Chinese ambassador should have dispelled them. Even after the deposition of the Emperor, the presentation of credentials had remained a simple ceremony attended by the Chairman of the PMAC, one or other of the Vice Chairmen and a few dignitaries. It normally rated two paragraphs in the press. On December 17, however, the entire Military Council had been summoned to the National Palace where, amid the kind of pomp previously associated with the Emperor, the new Chinese ambassador was officially received and his credentials accepted. Next day it was the lead story in *The Ethiopian Herald*. The ambassador, Mr. Yang Shou Chang, was quoted as saying that Ethiopia and China had a lot in common and were engaged 'in the fight against imperialism and colonialism'.

It was the kind of terminology we were to hear increasingly.

11 Unity or Death

A 'fallacious report' (December 18-22)

Late on the night of Sunday, December 22 Eritrean guerillas entered the provincial capital, Asmara, and launched a surprise attack on military installations. At least six government soldiers died and twenty were wounded in a night punctuated by machine-gun-fire and explosions. A similar attack was made on the port of Assab.

Since the beginning of December there had been a series of incidents in the province, the most important being the shooting and seriously wounding of the assistant provincial governor in the centre of the city on December 10. Most of the skirmishes were taking place in the countryside, the traditional 'battleground' of the secessionist forces, although tension had been building up in Asmara as more and more government troops arrived from Addis.

However, the attack that Sunday night was one of the most daring so far undertaken by the guerillas, whose leaders had been given new encouragement by open support from Arab countries – notably Kuwait, whose leaders had bluntly told a delegation from the Dergue that Ethiopia should 'follow the example of Portugal' and grant independence to its 'colonies'.

On Monday, December 23, maintaining the pretence of 'peace and tranquillity', the PMAC announced a new list of public holidays, replacing some Christian festivals by Moslem ones.

The announcement of the new holidays was also used as an excuse for public attacks on radio and in the press on the Orthodox

Church, which was accused of being responsible for holding back progress in Ethiopia.

Following the guerilla attack on Asmara, there was a series of murders of young people in the city. On Christmas night twenty bodies were found. All were young men in their twenties, mostly students, and all had been garotted with piano wire. Another eighteen were found on December 26, bringing the total over Christmas to fifty. None of the dead students was known to have any connection with the ELF, but they had died during the hours of curfew and reports from Asmara suggested that government forces were raiding homes and picking on anyone remotely likely to have ELF sympathies. Students were an obvious target.

There were also reports that hundreds of ordinary citizens were being arrested — some figures put the number as high as seven hundred — and Asmara was seething with a mixture of fear and anger. Civil leaders demanded that the PMAC do something, and on December 28 several officers of the Dergue, together with Information Minister Michael Imru, went to Asmara. At a meeting attended by more than two hundred religious, tribal and civic leaders, the PMAC delegation was told in no uncertain terms that their strong-arm approach to the Eritrean situation would achieve nothing. Several Eritrean leaders openly harangued the Dergue, and demanded that negotiations be opened with the ELF. After two days of straight talking, the Dergue leaders agreed that a committee of about thirty Eritrean leaders should be set up and given authority to make exploratory approaches to the secessionists with a view to preparing the way to top-level negotiations.

Meanwhile, back in Addis the authorities launched attacks on foreign news media, particularly the German station, Deutsche Welle, and the BBC. Correspondents for these media were accused of 'daily feeding the world with fallacious reports'. In particular the *Herald* criticized coverage recent events in Asmara: 'No amount of distortion of the facts can hide the real truth, no matter how hard certain detractors may try ... certain agents of imperialism are frantically trying to sow seeds of discord among Ethiopians by fabricating non-existing stories.'

The attack on the Western media and foreign correspondents was in fact just one aspect of a growing propaganda campaign against foreigners generally, and Europeans and Americans in particular.

The general attitude of the government was underlined on December 28 when orders were given to Radio Ethiopia to cancel its French language programmes and severely curtail its English ones, and Ethiopian TV was told to chop all Western TV shows. Instead, the evening's screen was filled with socialist documentaries produced in China and North Korea. References to the Vietnam War in news broadcasts spoke of the Communist forces as 'brave fighters of the Vietnamese revolution'.

Meanwhile I was having my own problems. I had more than suspected for some time that my telephone was being tapped. I had reason to believe my movements were being closely watched. And I knew my mail was being tampered with. It came to a head in the last three weeks in December when I spent a considerable amount of time – not exactly willingly – inside the Grand Palace HQ of the Dergue. Most of what went on will have to remain untold for the moment for the sake of others. Suffice to say that, seated in ornate chairs which still bore Emperor Haile Selassie's monogram, officers of the Dergue and I faced each other for many hours across a succession of tables. Everything I said on each occasion was carefully written down as I spoke. It must have made very boring reading.

I was first of all suspected of being a CIA agent. I was then accused of having returned from my June visit to Somalia to act as an agent of the Somali government. Finally, I was accused of being a 'link-man' for the ELF. My interrogaters were polite, even pleasant. They had a rather large dossier with my name on it, containing photographs, information about meetings I had had with various Ethiopian officials, statements about me from other Ethiopians – and some documents relating to the ELF which I had picked up in Somalia at the OAU meeting. These documents were in fact attacks on the Haile Selassie regime and as such should have been inoffensive to the Dergue, but obviously weren't.

In the middle of this period of interrogation, my wife and family left Ethiopia. Again, for the sake of others the exact details must remain undisclosed for the time being. But a number of threatening letters and phone calls and some unpleasant incidents directed against my family had built up to a situation in which it became advisable to send them back to England, for a time at least.

Snapping Threads (January 1-3 1975)

On January 1 the Military Council took their Ethiopian socialism a stage further with the announcement of the nationalization of all banks, finance houses and insurance companies. (Compensation was promised 'in the future' but at the time of writing has still not materialized.)

The nationalization announcement – apart from frightening off foreign investment – was an excellent illustration of the Dergue's desperate anxiety to introduce socialist measures, whether they understood and knew how to implement them or not. Only a week before, the Military Council had set up a committee of civilian experts and entrusted them with the task of drawing up a programme of nationalization – some two hundred companies and organizations were suggested – and of preparing a report on how it could be implemented. The Committee had barely started work, and were as surprised as anyone by the sudden announcement.

The same day, the students taking part in the Zemecha were put on a 24-hour standby, and told to prepare to leave for the countryside. Advance parties had already gone to the remoter areas to establish bases from which students would fan out to give instruction to the peasants in reading, writing and basic farming skills. In some areas, however, local leaders had already let it be known that the students would not be welcome.

Meanwhile a new source of opposition was developing. The outlawed governor of Tigre, Ras Mengesha Seyoum, had been quietly building up a small private army and had formed what he called 'The Front for the Liberation of Tigre'. At the beginning of January it was learned that he had been joined – at least in his opposition to the Dergue – by the equally outlawed governor of the north-west province of Begemdir and Simen, General Nege

137

Tegegne, who had supported the Dergue under Aman Andom and even addressed 'Ethiopia Tikdem' rallies in his province. But, like Ras Mengesha, he was married to a grand-daughter of Haile Selassie, and after Bloody Saturday she had been arrested and was being held with the other princesses and many of the children of the executed and detained aristocrats and ministers.

Neither of them could possibly hope, even by joining forces, to stand against the Ethiopian army. But they could have considerable nuisance value, especially, as was being suggested, if they agreed to work with the ELF.

There had also been reports from the eastern province of Harar that the Western Somali Liberation Front was active and had been attacking military vehicles on exposed roads near the border. And in the north-eastern area occupied by the Afars and Denakils – territories which had never been more than nominally part of Ethiopia – the ruling Sheikh, Ali Mira, was reported to be determined that they would stay that way.

In short, by early January there was trouble – real or potential – on every hand. The thin threads which had kept Ethiopia together during the revolution until the overthrow of the Emperor and immediately after, were now snapping one by one.

The Dergue had none but itself to blame. Its volatile mixture of ill-conceived and hastily introduced measures, based on false concepts of socialism and introduced by men following less an ideology than its attendant slogans, was fast bringing the country to the brink of chaos.

The killing of Aman Andom and the executions had had an unsettling effect on the whole country, and had alienated much of the goodwill hitherto shown to the Ethiopian revolutionaries by other countries.

Nationalization had made the business and commerce community apprehensive. An attempt at price controls – turning the clock back ten years – had resulted in the refusal of farmers to bring produce into the market places, creating shortages of basic foodstuffs such as grain and eggs and causing discontent in the cities. Attempts to appease the Moslems by granting them a few holidays had been

138

done in such a gauche way that it had alienated the Orthodox community. At least half the students due to take part in the Zemecha had 'defected', and many of the others were less than enthusiastic.

And, most decisive of all, there was the intransigence shown by the Dergue to the Eritrean situation – after hopes had been raised under General Aman that, for the first time in years, there might be a negotiated settlement.

The situation seemed to be neatly summed up, once again, by my Ethiopian friend: 'Ethiopia has become a schizophrenic with paranoid tendencies. It doesn't need a politician. It needs a psychiatrist.'

The Smouldering North (January 4-29)

When Information Minister Michael Imru had returned from his meeting with the Eritrean community and religious leaders he had brought with him a list of five demands which the committee of Eritrean representatives said must be fulfilled before they would assist the government.

On January 4 the Minister returned to Asmara to give the government's reply, and, after a night punctuated by a grenade attack on the city, the PMAC issued a statement on January 5. For the first time they used the word 'insurgents' in reference to the ELF instead of the usual 'bandits', and said that the previous 'harsh and oppressive regime' had forced many Eritreans to engage in armed struggle or flee the country. Now the government had talked to Eritrean leaders who had made some suggestions which would help in finding a settlement.

The government's version of these suggestions was: 'normalization of tight security measures imposed on Asmara as a result of last week's bomb explosion': the granting of amnesty to political prisoners in Eritrea as part of a nationwide amnesty; the making of 'special arrangements' for the National Work Campaign in Eritrea as most districts of the province were under emergency regulations, and the exercising of 'restraint in the activities of the

139

security forces in view of the peaceful discussions now going on'. The statement added that 'the Eritrean representatives have asked for permission to convey to the insurgents the goodwill of the PMAC and have pledged that they will do their best to prevent acts of violence'. The representatives had also asked that Eritrean community and religious leaders should take part in any negotiations 'between the government and the refugees abroad'.

The PMAC's reply, said the communiqué, was that 'the relevant authorities' had been directed to 'normalize' security measures and exercise maximum restraint on the activity of the security forces'; community elders had been authorized to contact insurgents and convey to them the need for a peaceful solution; subsequent talks between representatives of the government 'and prominent Eritrean leaders' would include religious and community leaders; all political prisoners would be 'considered for amnesty or reduction of prison terms' except those charged with murder and serious criminal offences, and the National Work Campaign had been told 'to take steps to make special arrangements'.

The replies didn't quite match up even to the government's version of the Eritreans' demands. In fact, the whole statement was a travesty of the truth. What the Eritrean committee had demanded was the total withdrawal of Ethiopian troops from the streets of Asmara; the opening of direct negotiations between the government and the ELF; the complete cancellation of the Zemecha in Eritrea; the *immediate* release of *all* Eritrean political prisoners; and – the fifth demand, not mentioned at all by the government statement – freedom of the press so that all news about Eritrea would be published nationally.

Over the next few days the ELF stepped up their attacks throughout Eritrea and leaders of the movement in Cairo and Beirut made it clear that Eritrean independence was 'not negotiable'. By Friday, January 10, guerillas had again attacked Asmara, causing grenade damage to the Town Hall, radio station and the offices of the USIS.

That night the military government issued a hurt and petulant statement. They were struggling to form a new kind of government and reshape the administration which had been responsible for Eritrea's ills. But there was a 'handful of people who allege to represent the people of Eritrea, but in reality are pursuing personal interests at the expense of the Eritrean masses'.

The same evening it was announced that Michael Imru had left to tour Arab countries. It was to prove an unrewarding trip, starting in Cairo, where the late General Aman's brother, the Ethiopian ambassador to Egypt, had just been granted political asylum, and from where the Arab League had just issued a statement indicating that it had been approached by the ELF for more support and a request that the League take up the Eritrean case with the OAU.

The Ethiopian government's statement that Friday evening had ended with what it called 'a final warning' to the 'irresponsible insurgents' in Eritrea. This ultimatum drew an immediate reaction from the ELF, whose Foreign Affairs spokesman issued a statement the next day reaffirming that talks could only begin when the military rulers recognized the province's right to independence.

Meanwhile the committee of Eritrean community and religious leaders had split into two groups, one talking to the ELF and the other to the breakaway, Marxist-orientated PLF. But instead of persuading either group to negotiate with the central government, the committee's efforts succeeded in uniting the two previously rival liberation movements to fight under one banner. On January 15 leaders of the two groups signed a formal accord. It was probably the single most significant event to date in the prolonged guerilla war in the province.

On the evening of January 15 the government issued another warning to the guerillas. The patience of the PMAC, it said, should not be taken as a sign of weakness. The people of the province were falling into 'an imperialist trap'. Eritrea, it added, was Ethiopia, and Ethiopia was Eritrea. It didn't leave much room for negotiation.

That Friday's *Addis Zemen* — the Amharic language newspaper which reflected and often 'predicted' government policy and action — had launched its strongest attack on foreigners in Ethiopia, saying that more than threequarters of them were not needed and that their jobs would be given to Ethiopians. It singled out what it called 'capitalist expatriates' – presumably so as not to offend the increasing number of Chinese and Russians in the country.

All was far from well within the Dergue itself, however. Since Bloody Saturday, the military committee had been slowly shrinking as one after another the more moderate officers disappeared – mainly of their own free will. By mid-January it was estimated that only about eighty members were left of the original hundred and twenty. Even within this reduced group, however, divisions had been developing. Since the 'Zemecha Day' parade when he had been so enthusiastically cheered, Mengistu was reported to have been trying to set himself up as the real leader of the government.

On November 19 he had been named officially by Radio Ethiopia as 'the patriot and officer of great courage' who had been behind the coup that overthrew Haile Selassie, and there was talk that General Teferi might be asked to make way for Mengistu. There was little doubt that he would, without objection. But the Second Vice Chairman of the Dergue, Major Atenafu, had other ideas. He thought none of the key members of the Dergue should, for the moment anyway, take over the leadership. In any case, since Major Atenafu was believed to be the real 'brains' behind the socialist – now increasingly Communist – programme, it is likely that if anyone was to replace the General, Major Atenafu considered that he was that person.

In any event, the situation became so serious that at the end of the third week in January the two men had lined up their supporters and there was a real threat of the whole military government collapsing. As this would leave the Eritreans and all the other rebel groups – not to mention the Somalis – with no organized opposition, the two men were persuaded by a number of uncommitted officers to have a talk with, of all people, the Patriarch of the Orthodox Church, Abune Tewoflos. The Abune was apparently successful in persuading the two men that their only hope of survival lay in working together, though it is likely that the growing pressure of the country's other problems had as much influence in keeping what was left of the Dergue together as anything the Patriarch said.

Law and order in the countryside were breaking down. Impatient peasants in the south were grabbing land they felt was theirs regardless of any land reform proposals, and the Zemecha was running into trouble. On January 22 reports reached the capital that a number of students had been shot and others attacked and injured by angry peasants in Sidamo and Gemu Gofa provinces. Camps built for the student workers had been burned down in some places, and a group of students was returning to Addis with reports of bad organization, lack of food and water, and peasant resistance.

At Lalibella, site of the famous rock churches, some tourists had had a narrow escape when an Ethiopian Airlines plane was, at the last moment before landing, 'waved over' by police, who found that ditches had been dug across the airstrip and then camouflaged.

Meanwhile the Lutheran-backed Radio Voice of the Gospel had become the subject of attacks in the press and on the state radio station. RVOG had always operated under some restrictions imposed by the Haile Selassie regime as a condition of its existence in Ethiopia. These restrictions had increased in direct ratio to the military's increasing hold on the country, and since the overthrow of Haile Selassie, RVOG's entire news and current affairs operation had been under total censorship. In view of the station's supposedly independent nature, and particularly its professed Christian commitment, the Lutheran World Federation Broadcasting Service in Geneva, which had oversight of the operation, requested a top-level meeting with the government. But when Geneva announced to the world's press that it was seeking such a meeting, RVOG's news services were ordered to delete the references in the statement to difficulties being experienced in covering the Ethiopian situation. (At the time of writing, RVOG is still broadcasting under the same restrictions, and still trying to clarify its position.)

Eritrea was still the main area of activity, however, and there had been no let-up by the guerillas. On January 25 the ELF conducted a daring daylight raid on the main traffic police HQ in Asmara. A group of guerillas burst into the building and kidnapped a number of police officers. The government was stunned into issuing a statement about the incident that night, describing the guerillas as 'misguided elements'. No immediate represals would be taken, said the statement, because of the desire to protect innocent civilians. It was all part of their attempt to win public sympathy from the rest of Ethiopia. (The statement included an attack on Deutsche Welle and the BBC, denying that there was any opposition to the Zemecha and adding that it was 'regrettable that some foreign correspondents should fall victim to vicious rumours put about by people opposed to Ethiopian socialism'. It was becoming clear my days in Ethiopia were numbered.)

Another ELF attack destroyed a convoy of fuel tankers on the road inland from Assab, and on the evening of January 28 the government, quite uncharacteristically, announced this fact in a 'newsflash' on the radio. A few minutes later, the government issued another 'final warning' to the guerillas: 'Woe to those bandits and their leaders who repeatedly try to disrupt public order.' It went on to say that Ethiopia 'now demands the hands of her true and vigilant sons to suppress bandit elements', and that the government had 'reached the final point of restraint' and would now proceed to 'eliminate those who dream of Ethiopia's disunity'.

It was, to all intents and purposes, a call to arms and a declaration of war.

Asmara Offensive (January 31 – February 5)
Under cover of darkness and the dense fog that often shrouds Asmara at that time of year, an ELF guerilla force slipped into the city just before 7 pm on the evening of Friday, January 31, and took up positions in streets around the main Second Division HQ.

A few minutes later, using machine-guns, mortars and bazookas, they launched the strongest and boldest attack of the thirteen-year guerilla war, firing directly into the barracks. A few minutes after this attack started, another was launched on the Ethiopian Navy HQ and on the northern headquarters of the Imperial Bodyguard.

Five hours later the battle was still going on, intermittently, in various parts of the city.

After a brief lull, the fighting resumed the following morning. A few shops had opened when the curfew ended at 7 am, and a few residents had appeared on the streets. But within an hour a series of explosions sent people scurrying for shelter.

Reports reaching Addis by the microwave telephone link said civilian casualties appeared to be heavy. An eyewitness said that he had counted twenty bodies, mostly civilians, sprawled in the street outside his home near the Second Division barracks, and another resident reported counting a pile of sixteen bodies in a ditch near the airport.

Radio Ethiopia, however, merely made a brief statement that in Asmara, security forces were 'on the alert after a handful of bandits opened fire in an effort to disrupt public order'.

Later that afternoon many civilian casualties were reported when government troops using heavy artillery bombarded two villages to the north of Asmara. It is doubtful whether there was a single guerilla in either of the villages by that time, but the troops were out for revenge. The previous day, a few hours before the initial guerilla attack on Asmara, a Second Division patrol had been ambushed and virtually wiped out by an ELF unit between these villages, and the government forces suspected the villagers had been hiding and supporting the guerillas.

Early that evening fighting resumed in Asmara itself and one British resident who had managed to travel about a hundred yards from his home before being forced back by sniper fire reported that the government troops appeared to be out of control and to be firing wildly at anything that moved.

His impression was reinforced later on Saturday night with telephoned reports from Asmara of troops, ostensibly on a house-to-house search for insurgents, bursting into homes and shooting indiscriminately into cupboards and through closed bedroom doors.

The government forces weren't having it all their own way, however. The original order for the search-and-destroy mission had been given to the Asmara police. But a few days before, the Commander-General of the Eritrean Police, General Goitem Gebre-Egzy, had defected to the ELF, taking with him some special

145

police commanders – who had been given intensive training in guerilla tactics to fight against the ELF!

With their leader gone, and their loyalty as Eritreans overcoming their allegiance to the Ethiopian government, many of the police had first refused to carry out the orders, and then defected. Some of the sporadic shooting heard in the city in those first forty-eight hours was, in fact, between soldiers and police who had switched to the ELF cause.

A number of Second Division troops were also reported to have defected to the guerillas, and the government ran into trouble with an order to the air force to start bombarding villages suspected of harbouring secessionist forces. A high proportion of the air force personnel were Eritrean or Tigrean. Several air crew refused to bomb their own people, some had been arrested, and others had managed to escape from Debre Zeit.

The government were also facing armed opposition in Tigre and Begemdir from Ras Mengesha and General Nege, who were reported to have between them about 20,000 men capable of putting up armed resistance. And a quite separate little 'war' was going on only eighty miles north of Addis Ababa where the sons of a prominent Shoan nobleman, Ras Biru Wolde-Gebriel, were holding out in some caves with a few hundred supporters after fighting off government troops trying to take over their land on behalf of the government.

The main reason, however, for the lack of cohesion of the government forces in the north was that the entire northern committee of the Dergue had flown to Addis just before the fighting started for a series of meetings with the central Co-ordinating Committee. The purpose of these meetings was to plan a major offensive against the ELF forces, timed, it was understood, to begin that weekend. But the ELF had learned of the plan, and their attack on Asmara had not been intended to capture it, but to pre-empt the government offensive by creating as much confusion as possible.

On Friday, however, just as the attack was starting, the ELF were given every reason to believe that they now had nothing to lose by continuing the fighting. Michael Imru, then in Damascus on his abortive Arab tour, had stated categorically that Ethiopia's military rulers would never grant independence to Eritrea.

Explanation – And Exit (February 1-5)

It was a far cry from Aman Andom's conciliatory language. What had brought about the change? The only real clue to this so far lies in the admittedly circumstantial evidence of an increased Chinese presence in the country, Chinese and North Korean programmes on TV, articles about China in the press, Major Atenafu's association with China, the fuss made of the new Chinese ambassador, the sudden increase in Ethiopian Airlines direct flights to Peking from one to two a week, and the Maoist-style propaganda used to put forward the Dergue's socialist ideas.

The amount of anti-Western propaganda and communist slogans had grown in direct ratio to this increased emphasis on things Chinese, and several leftist extremists I talked to told me unashamedly after Bloody Saturday that it was the 'Chinese revolutionary way' to 'eliminate all reactionary forces'.

The Chinese interest in Eritrea lay in its 'cold war' with the Soviet Union and in the fact that with the imminent opening of the Suez canal, the Red Sea had increased considerably in strategic importance as a route for Russian vessels into the Indian Ocean. The Russians already had at least highly-developed facilities, if not an actual base, at Berbera on the Gulf of Aden coast of Somalia (a contributing factor to America's desire to expand its base on the British-owned Indian Ocean island of Diego Garcia).

The Chinese are believed to want similar facilities in the area, and their influence in Ethiopia would be of considerably less use if the country did not retain control of its Red Sea coastline.

The Arabs, on the other hand, are known to want control of the whole of the Red Sea, and this is thought to be the main reason behind their overwhelming support of the ELF.

Caught in the middle of this power game were – and are – the Americans, still with the remnants of a communications base at Kagnew in Asmara, still with their Military Assistance and Advisory

147

Group headquarters in Addis Ababa, and still officially supplying arms to Ethiopia. Their obligation to the Ethiopian government meant, in effect, that they would be assisting the fight against Eritrean secessionists. And that would put them in opposition to the Arab world. On the other hand, to cancel agreements and pull out of Ethiopia would leave the Chinese a clear run. (In fact, it seems as if Washington has decided to hold its ground. On January 5 the Americans filled a two-year vacancy in Addis Ababa by appointing as ambassador Mr. Arthur Hummel, a career diplomat who just happens to have been born and educated in China, speaks several dialects fluently, and was one of the State Department's leading experts on East Asian affairs.)

On Sunday, February 2 two Ethiopian air force fighter bombers began strafing and bombing villages around Asmara, causing heavy casualties, while guerilla units blew up electricity and water supply installations, and in spite of a statement from the ELF that the weekend's activities were designed only as a show of strength, it was obvious that the guerilla war had moved out of its hit-and-run phase and into a new, more direct form of conflict.

Estimates of guerilla strength varied wildly, but were reliably put at 5,000 trained fighting men and up to 20,000 'irregulars' — who would be of little use in open conflict around Asmara, but could maintain the more usual guerilla tactics in the countryside. In fact, this is what they were doing, and they had already taken control of the roads leading to Asmara from Addis, Massawa and Assab.

A convoy of troops trying to reach the north by way of Mekele was virtually wiped out, and another convoy of tanks, half-tracks and troops sent up from Addis was stopped when guerillas blew up several bridges on the Addis-Asmara road about eighty miles south of the northern city. The convoy was ambushed and attacked, and only about five of a reported fifty vehicles eventually made it to Asmara, where the situation was such that embassies had started evacuation of their nationals.

A few weeks before, my colleague Bill Lee, who like me had been involved in interrogation sessions by military security convinced that all American journalists were CIA agents, had been given a warning that he might be arrested and had left Ethiopia. A few days later, security forces had come to arrest him, and had been more than slightly put out to discover he had gone. At the same time they had inquired if I was still in Ethiopia and had indicated that they would probably be returning for me.

I decided it was time to make discretion the better part of valour, and calculating that with the government in its present state of confusion the right hand would not know what the left hand was doing, I applied for permission to leave the country (foreign residents require exit visas just like Ethiopian Nationals).

My application lay untouched for some days, then, suddenly, almost the entire clerical and administrative staff of the Immigration Department — many of them Eritreans and Tigreans — was changed overnight. In the confusion, and in spite of the fact that the military security had made it clear that they weren't finished with me, I was granted a visa — although only after a bond of E$10,000 (£2,000) was posted guaranteeing my return!

My plans to leave were accelerated, however, when information reached me just before the fighting started in Asmara that a group of extremists — believed to be the Ethiopian National Front which had previously sent me a threatening letter — had plans to kidnap me, and, so the story went, to arrange an 'accident'.

Then, on the night of Saturday, February 1, word reached me from Europe that the Russian News Agency, TASS, had issued a story that I had been arrested and was about to be deported. It was either wishful thinking or they knew something I didn't!

The next afternoon, in a report to the BBC I included the information that 'the government is known to have set up at least three major concentration camps around Addis and to have plans to round up and detain thousands of Eritreans in the capital if the situation in the north deteriorates further'. (In fact the round-up had already started, and was one of the reasons behind the sudden purge in the immigration department.)

My report, however, caused something of a stir in government circles. It also annoyed some journalist colleagues who expressed open disbelief. (It was to be small consolation that within a week

149

street-fighting had erupted in parts of the capital as Eritreans put up armed resistance to being taken to the camps, which by this time housed scores whose detention had already been effected.)

It was now a question of who would get to me first – the government to deport me, or the extremist group to arrange a nasty accident!

On Monday, foreign nationals began being airlifted from Asmara – not without some interference from the Ethiopian government. One of two specially chartered planes sent to Asmara was immediately impounded by the military and used to fly out officers' wives and children. French military authorities in Djibouti sent two planes in, and when one of them arrived at Addis Ababa late on Tuesday, the airport authorities switched off the landing lights. It took more than half an hour of angry and intense diplomatic activity to persuade the control tower to allow the plane to land.

By Tuesday evening the death toll in the fighting in and around Asmara stood at about fifteen hundred – mostly civilians; electricity and water supplies were virtually non-existent; food stocks were running low; there was a real fear of outbreaks of cholera and typhoid in the city; and some Ethiopian Airlines regular service flights were being cancelled and the planes commandeered to take troops and ammunition to the north.

The government, too, was feeling the strain. One of the key members of the Dergue, Eritrean-born Major Michael Gebre Negus, who had been a member of a touring delegation to Algeria and Tunisia in December to explain the policies of the military government, had defected that day to the ELF. And the recently-appointed Minister of Agriculture, Dr Dagnatchew Yirgu, had disappeared, reportedly to seek asylum in the Sudan.

On the afternoon of Wednesday, February 5 as American, British Indian, Greek and Italian evacuees – some, taken from hospitals, still in their pyjamas – were being loaded onto refugee planes in Asmara, I was boarding a Cairo-bound plane in Addis.

A few hours later, flying over Asmara at 30,000 feet, long tongues of flame and thick clouds of smoke could be seen spiralling up from villages around the city. I don't mind confessing that there were tears in my eyes. For me, the revolution was over. But for twenty-six million Ethiopians it had only just begun.

Postcript (February 6 – May 1)

Since I left Ethiopia, the Military Government's dislike of the truth being spread abroad has continued with the expulsion of the representatives of the two major Western news agencies, Agence France Presse (AFP) and Reuter. Meanwhile, the situation has remained extremely volatile.

There is no sign of a softening in the government's attitude to the Eritrean issue since a toughly-worded broadcast from Major Mengistu on February 7 called for 'unity or death', and said the government considered Ethiopia's unity 'inviolate'.

Throughout Ethiopia there is considerable unrest and tension and the military government is reported to be in a very unstable position with internal divisions and external opposition, mainly as a result of a declaration of land nationalization. The second Division has also demanded that the government open negotiations with the ELF, and a number of plots against the Dergue have been foiled. Land nationalization has been welcomed in some areas, but in others landlords have been putting up armed resistance to government forces.

On March 5 the PMAC announced a reshuffle of civilian positions in the cabinet. One-time Prime Minister and, since September 12, Information Minister and not-too-successful roving ambassador of the Military Council, Michael Imru was redesignated Chief Political Adviser in the office of the Chairman of the PMAC.

Meanwhile Haile Selassie is reported to be well cared for in his Palace prison, and to be taking an active interest in the progress of the revolution. But the military's outward flirtation with the idea of constitutional monarchy was officially broken off on March 21 with a proclamation revoking the invitation to Crown Prince Asfa Wossen to return and be crowned king, and abolishing the monarchy altogether.

151

12 The Headless Chicken

(An Opinion)

Conclusions

Only the week before I left Ethiopia, a missionary friend in Addis Ababa had a visit from some tribesmen he had worked among some time before. They had travelled for days over some of the wildest territory in Ethiopia to find out what was going on. Their first question to the missionary was: 'Is it true that the Emperor is involved in a power struggle with one of his grandsons?'

The story sums up the problem of Ethiopia and its revolution. For although it had been going on for a year, although the military government issued proclamations in the name of the 'broad masses of the Ethiopian people', Ethiopia's revolution had touched barely a fraction of the population.

Which is not to detract from the unarguably high ideals of the revolutionaries. But just living from day to day was problem enough for most people, who, even in the towns, were at most little more than spectators of the Creeping Coup. The active ones were the traditional dissenters — students, intellectuals, teachers, the tiny labour movement — and in no way could it be called a 'revolution of the people'.

Nor, of course, was it true that the masses were fanatical supporters of Haile Selassie. That was a myth encouraged by the Emperor himself, and swallowed all too easily by his friends abroad.

The masses accepted their conditions almost fatalistically. It took the military to make them see that a better life was possible.

In an article discussing the Eritrean situation in *New Middle East* in April 1971, Graham Tayar, an observer and analyst of Ethiopian affairs, concluded: 'What is critical, not for the ELF ... but for the survival of the [Haile Selassie] regime is what is happening today among the younger and more radical officers in the Ethiopian armed forces.'

What had been happening, and continued to happen, came to the surface in an eruption of discontent and anger in February 1974. The catalyst was the civil unrest resulting from economic pressures. The support came from the traditional civilian radicals.

If the aristocrats, ministers and officials had stuck together, they might have been able to fend off the inevitable for perhaps a few more years. But each was too busy trying to take advantage of the situation to realize that it was not just individuals who were being attacked, as in the past, but the very system they represented.

One important factor in the maintenance of the Haile Selassie regime – as it had been of previous regimes – was that aspect of the Ethiopian character, born of centuries of tradition, which needed some figure at the top whom they could fear, even if they could not love. Haile Selassie was the only unifying force the country knew. The end of his system was inevitable, and, with the slightest nudge from the military, it finally collapsed in on itself.

The revolutionaries were then faced with a dilemma. All that they wished to destroy was embodied in the person of the Emperor. Logic dictated that he, too, would have to be removed. Instinct, however, told many of the members of the Dergue that there was a very real danger that his removal would lead to the disintegration of Ethiopia's fragile unity.

Even so, and much to the surprise of many observers, under Aman Andom it looked as though an Emperor-less Ethiopia might survive intact. But when the hard-liners under Mengistu and Atenafu took control of the movement, killed Aman, massacred the ministers and tried to drag their country into some instant socialist Utopia, they betrayed the truly socialist and altruistic aims of the

153

Ethiopia Tikdem message, and replaced Haile Selassie's despotic feudalism with an equally rigid doctrinaire militarist tryanny. Ethiopia was left after November 23, as I put it in a BBC despatch, with all the grace, dignity and sense of direction of a headless chicken.

And the long-feared post-Haile Selassie fragmentation of the Ethiopian Empire began.

The Future

In a report I sent from Cairo on February 6 1975 for the BBC's programme 'From Our Own Correspondent', I commented: 'It's always sad to hear of a dream being shattered. But it's sadder still to have lived in such a dream as an observer; to have seen hope transformed into enthusiasm; to have witnessed a people drained of initiative by centuries of feudalism, stir themselves and clutch at a dream of freedom, and then to see the dream that almost became a reality, crumble to dust even as they grasped it ... It's a sad story. Saddest of all for the millions of ordinary Ethiopians who, almost exactly a year after the dawn of hope, have little to look forward to except the darkness of increased chaos.'

Looking back, I think I might have been somewhat pessimistic – although little has happened since to justify any optimism.

True, at the moment, Ethiopia is leaderless; its people divided against themselves; its rulers relying on the doubtful unity of the armed forces and the even more doubtful support of urban radicals for the most part determined to see civilian rule; and its economy drifting remorselessly towards disaster. But Ethiopia has been through all this before, and survived.

Embodied in the revolution, and beginning to be put into effect, clumsily, by the military government, are the seeds of hope for the future – land reform, plans for improved housing, a fairer taxation system.

In their proclamation abolishing the monarchy, the PMAC concluded with the promise: 'After organizing themselves ... the people will set up a people's government in which they will be their own masters. Ethiopia First. May socialism flourish.'

If this promise is kept, and given leaders rather than taskmasters, this can still be achieved. If it isn't — and if the cellars of the National Palace and other places of detentions remain filled with people who have been held, in some cases for a year, without trial, and without hope of a fair hearing — the 'glory of Ethiopia', as the *Accra Guardian* put it, will be lost forever, and a beautiful country and its people will suffer for many years to come.

BIBLIOGRAPHY

Books and pamphlets

Abir, Mordecai. 'The Contentious Horn of Africa'. *Conflict Studies* (London, June 1972)

Atkins, Harry. *A History of Ethiopia* (Addis Ababa, 1968)

Clapham, Christopher. *Haile Selassie's Government* (London, 1969)

Doresse, Jean. *Histoire Sommaire de la Corne Orientale de l'Afrique* (Paris, 1971)

Ethiopian Information Ministry. *Biography of an Idea — Story of a Vision Achieved* (Addis Ababa, 1969, 1973)

Gilkes, Patrick. *The Dying Lion: Feudalism and Modernization in Ethiopia* (London, 1975)

Greenfield, Richard. *Ethiopia: A New Politcal History* (London, 1965)

Legum, Colin. 'The Future of Ethiopia'. *Year Book of World Affairs,* Vol. 28 (London 1974)

Levine, D. *Wax and Gold* (Chicago, 1966)

Perham, M. *The Government of Ethiopia* (London, 1969)

Tayar, Graham. 'Ethiopia's Rebellion'. *Africa Report,* Vol. XIV, No. 8 (London 1969)

Tayar, Graham. 'Rebellion in Eritrea: Who is behind it? What are its aims?' *New Middle East* (London, April 1971)

Other sources

Africa Research Bulletin (May 1974 — January 1975)

BBC Monitoring Service: *Summary of World Broadcasts — Part 4 Middle East and Africa* (March, April 1975)

The Ethiopian Herald (January — December 1974; January, February 1975)

Numerous unpublished documents obtained from the armed forces, Ethiopian students' and teachers' organizations, the Eritrean Liberation Front, the Western Somali Liberation Front, the Oromo Liberation Movement, the Confederation of Ethiopian Labour Movement Unions (CELU).

INDEX

157

THE AUTHOR

Born in Scotland, Blair Thomson was a journalist on several newspapers before becoming associate editor of ATV's 'Today' programme. He then worked for BBC TV in Leeds and Sheffield. In 1973 he went to Addis Ababa as English News Editor with the Lutheran World Federation Broadcasting Service, and when the Revolution began a few weeks later, he covered events for the BBC, *Daily Express, Observer, Time Magazine*, ABC of America, etc. until forced to leave the country in February 1975 with a price on his head. He continues to contribute comment and analysis of the situation to newspapers and the BBC.